A REPUBLIC
BY THE PEOPLE

Praise for A **Republic By** the **People**

"With our democracy fissuring more and more in recent years, we need to abandon polarized thinking, work together as one, and begin to heal our republic. Bill Bivins offers a path forward."
— David Aretha, award-winning author

"This book is a thoughtful and courageous look at the state of our country today—honest, informed, and deeply caring. It gave me new hope that we can find common ground and move forward together. I highly recommend it to anyone who wants to understand what's really at stake and how we can protect the values that matter most."
— Jane Vanderburgh, Senior Vice President, Sales

"Democracy and freedom are explained in detail—an excellent presentation that everyone should read. We should never forget the importance of these principles and how they shape our lives."
— Sandy Ringer, President, PHR / SHRM-CP,
Business Visions Consulting

"Bill Bivins takes the reader on a truly mind-opening view of today's political reality. His insight into what we the people can do to protect our republic is a must-read!"
— Trey Runyon, Director of Operations

"In *A Republic By The People*, Bill Bivins offers a centrist's solution which could serve as a compromise between the left and the right. It's a prescription to our current critical illness."
— John Davidson, retired math teacher

A **REPUBLIC** **BY** THE **PEOPLE**

A Common Sense Response to Project 2025

BILL BIVINS

BY
THE
PEOPLE
PRESS

For more information, or to contact the author about speaking or ordering books in bulk, visit www.linkedin.com/in/billbivins.

ISBN: 979-8-9986321-0-5 (paperback)
ISBN: 979-8-9986321-1-2 (hardcover)
ISBN: 979-8-9986321-2-9 (ebook)

Editor: David Aretha
Book design: Christy Day, Constellation Book Services
Author photo: Will Bivins

Library of Congress Control Number: 2025911149

Printed in the United States of America

For Americans whose love of country
puts principle before politics,
who reject division,
who believe in decency, in democracy, and in each other,
who still carry the quiet burden of keeping the Republic.
This book is for you —
the majority too often ignored,
the ones who choose a country that serves the people,
not the powerful,
and are willing to fight to restore what the Founders envisioned.

United we stand.

Contents

Author's Note

"A Republic, if you can keep it."

— BENJAMIN FRANKLIN

Franklin wasn't being clever—he was issuing a warning. What was created in Philadelphia was not a guarantee, but a gamble. A republic is not self-sustaining. It requires vigilance. It demands participation. And when threatened, it must be defended—not just by politicians or judges, but by the people themselves.

I didn't set out to write a book.

Like many Americans, I watched the 2016 presidential campaign with growing concern. The tribalism. The manipulation. The eerie echoes of history. I revisited two books I hadn't read since school—*1984* and *Mein Kampf*—and read them in parallel. The patterns were chillingly familiar.

As a veteran, an inventor, and a clean energy entrepreneur, I've spent my life building systems designed to serve the public good. But the system I saw unraveling before me wasn't about energy or infrastructure—it was the very architecture of democracy.

What began as a search for understanding turned into years of research into America's political history: how parties evolved, how public opinion was engineered, how fear and misinformation were weaponized. Along the way, I uncovered a deeply coordinated effort to reshape the American government in ways that benefit the few and silence the many.

Project 2025 is not just another policy platform. It is a plan to dismantle the republic—to replace the will of the people with the rule of ideology. It is, in no uncertain terms, a threat to our democracy.

This book is my response.

A Republic by the People: A Common Sense Response to Project 2025 is not a partisan argument. It is a patriotic one. It draws inspiration from the clarity and conviction of Thomas Paine's *Common Sense*—written not for scholars or strategists, but for ordinary citizens determined to shape their own destiny.

Each chapter is written for the people: the worker, the teacher, the student, the veteran, the parent, the voter. This is not about left or right. It's about whether we're still willing to show up—to speak out—to stand up for the Republic that was entrusted to us.

We are not powerless.

We are not alone.

And the Republic is still ours—if we choose to keep it.

—Bill Bivins

Preface

More in Common

For years, I have imagined creating guiding documents that can spark productive conversations on the biggest questions of our time. My goal is to go beyond partisanship and the cult of personality surrounding individual leaders or political parties. Instead, I will remind everyone about the basic rule that it is the government that must serve the people. The United States, this remarkable "great experiment," stands as an enduring testament to the possibilities of self-governance, balancing the individual's rights and the needs of the collective. But it is also an experiment that, like any experiment, will only thrive if there is vigilance, accountability, and the courage to adapt as the times and campaigns change.

But as I have talked with people of diverse political views and backgrounds, I have found a common hunger for solutions grounded in logic, fairness, and devotion to the common good. Though they view each other with visceral, interpersonal loathing over social issues, cultural issues, identity issues, lifestyle issues, and sex issues, there are still fundamental commonalities on crucial issues such as affordable healthcare, virtually sustainable economic opportunities, environmental stewardship, and ethical governance. Yet how to reach these agreed-upon goals is where most Americans cannot meet in the middle. These differences should not divide us; they should drive us toward rigorous debate and creative problem-solving. This document is an appeal to the moderate majority—a plea for principled governance, a demand to hold elected leaders to the same high ethical standards of integrity and decency that we have for ourselves.

This is not an attack on the greatness of our country or a proposal for a better solution than what is outlined in this Constitution. Instead, it respects the Founders' insight that perfection was an impossible ideal, that democracy was a living saga, with change and amendment, like renewal, essential to address a society's changing circumstances. Our Founders knew that our liberty and our justice must be renewed with each generation, for our country is only as strong as the values we instill in ourselves, each other, and our children. In this vein, it is written as a response to our moment, in which dysfunction, partisanship, and a marriage between the muscularity of power rather than the gentility of persuasion have eroded trust in institutions and corroded our public discourse.

The United States is so much more than borders, states, policies, or institutions—it is a principle of freedom and equality and justice and the pursuit of happiness. These principles, whether they apply one way or the other, are immune to political fashions or the personalities of any time. Yet, the ideals that have inspired us increasingly are drowned out by divisive rhetoric, ideological rigidity, and emotional manipulation. We cannot allow this trajectory to continue. The crises we face—climate change, systemic inequality, threats to democracy—require a unity of purpose and a restoration of the common values that bind us as a people.

This book is based on how men and women, some in America and others reacting to America, have led and challenged the American ethos: people such as Barry Goldwater, Dwight Eisenhower, Franklin D. Roosevelt, Martin Luther King Jr., Lyndon Johnson, Rachel Carson, George Will, Charles Krauthammer, and Ta-Nehisi Coates. It aims to remind readers that the tenets of justice, accountability, unity, and progress are not partisan but universal ones that have served this republic in its greatest crises. These words and ideas provide a working foundation for the road ahead—a road marked by courage, pragmatism, and abiding faith in the transformative power of people's will-based governance.

It is not just a romantic nostalgia for an imaginary golden age long gone; it is a challenge to face the moment with clarity, determination, and commitment to a common goal. This view also takes into account our past—both its flaws and its points of inspiration. But seeking a more perfect union demands that we realize the value of learning from the lessons of our history—in our successes and in our failures. And so let the building of the past guide us, not take us backward—but onward, toward an America where democracy is thriving, where the principles of our foundation are among the things we do not compromise.

Most importantly, this book is a call to Americans to take back the reins of our government. It is a call for us to rise above distractions and demagogic temptations, and to attain a clearer, more moral metric for ourselves and our elected officials. The solution does not reside in blind loyalty to a party or ideology, but rather in an unwavering commitment to the ideals of fairness, logic, and progress. It is not just a book at all, but a manifesto to restore the civic energies that have always been the heart of our republic.

I should share with you, as will be noted by those who find the opinions expressed objectionable, that I have neither an academic degree in politics nor have I served in political office. I have degrees—Nuclear Engineering, Propulsion Engineering, Economics, and Physics—just not politics. As an engineer and scientist, I like to look for logical, common-sense responses to problems. My lobbyist and politician friends remind me that applying logic to politics can be far too frustrating.

Bias Disclosure: My Beliefs Expressed in This Writing

I believe that the government plays a significant role in creating a fertile environment for economic prosperity and general welfare. It must ensure the rights of the individual are protected as strongly as those of the majority (or party in power). These ideas, proven over time, offer the best outcomes for most Americans.

I believe a patriot is willing to accept that our union is not perfect and address areas that need to be improved.

I believe a patriot is willing to challenge their party's leadership and often break from the party line.

I believe we have concentrated power in the hands of a few people.

We have ignored the Constitution and disregarded the principles of limited government.

I believe our great nation has an obligation to protect and care for its weakest members.

I believe in representation for taxation.

I believe the two-party system benefits from divisive rhetoric...a divided nation will eventually fall.

I believe in affordable healthcare for all in the United States.

I believe in equal treatment for all Americans, but preferential treatment for none regardless of economic or political stature.

I believe the government must enforce antitrust laws to protect consumers from predatory overbearing business monopolies, and greedflation, and ensure fair competition. Unionism in its proper sphere accomplishes a positive good for the country.

I believe in a sound Social Security system, and I want to see it strengthened.

I believe we must honor our U.S. military veterans. For them to rely on charity organizations to meet basic needs is disrespectful.

I believe government spending policies should be fiscally responsible and socially reasonable. Spending must be prioritized for the majority, not the elite minority.

I believe the U.S. government is currently controlled by a corporate oligarchy that perpetuates rigged capitalism where profits are privatized, and losses are socialized at the expense of taxpayers and the environment.

The Historical Roots of My Beliefs

At first glance, my beliefs may seem too liberal or even "woke" to some. Yet a close-up reveals them to be familiar ideas sprung from the philosophies and platforms of traditionally conservative leaders, innovators, and visionaries—people who have molded America's political, economic, and cultural fabric. These faiths—far from radical or new—harken back to values that have been the bedrock of the nation's growth and success.

Twentieth-Century Republican Leaders

Consider *Barry Goldwater's* presidential run in 1964. Better known for his staunch conservative views, Goldwater stressed limited government, personal freedoms, and a strong national defense. But he also respected personal liberties that could today be called progressive. Goldwater warned against government overreaching into private lives, famously saying, *"Extremism in the defense of liberty is no vice. And moderation in the pursuit of justice is no virtue."* His guidepost of principled conservatism contained an acknowledgment that liberty demands a balance of individual rights and collective responsibility—principles evident in my beliefs.

Likewise, Mitch McConnell's early Senate campaign in 1983–84 embodied a platform of pragmatism and institutional integrity. In particular, McConnell emphasized support for organized labor (AFL-CIO), economic development, government accountability, and investment in infrastructure, issues that, at the time, transcended partisan divides.[1] His legacy, though eclipsed later in life by an entirely different kind of politics, is a reminder that governance can, and should, be about solving problems, not ideology.

Abraham Lincoln: A Platform of Progress

Abraham Lincoln, widely considered the best president in American history, shaped his political career around a vision of minority rights, economic development, and innovation. His dedication to emancipation represented a deep-seated belief in the equality and dignity of all people, a sentiment that I hold dear. With labor and infrastructure at the forefront—his support for the transcontinental railroad and the Homestead Act, too—Lincoln recognized that progress in economic development held the promise of bridging a partisan divide and creating opportunities for every American.

Lincoln's legacy is a potent reminder that social justice, economic progress, and innovation policies are not intrinsically partisan. Rather, they are fundamental to the American experiment. His words "The dogmas of the quiet past are inadequate to the stormy present"[2] remind us that adaptability and progress are essential in meeting the challenges of each new era.

The Visionaries of Industry and Innovation

In the fullest sense of collective power, industrial pioneers like Henry Ford, Milton Hershey, and the Vanderbilt family embody forward-looking principles that balance economic prosperity and social benefit:

Henry Ford revolutionized manufacturing with the assembly line, democratizing access to goods like the automobile. But Ford's legacy extends beyond innovation—he famously raised wages for his workers, understanding that economic growth was sustainable only when shared with the people who helped create it. His belief in a symbiotic relationship between labor and capital resonates with modern calls for economic equity and workers' rights.[3,4]

Milton Hershey's legacy exemplifies how businesses can drive social good alongside profit. He founded the town of Hershey, Pennsylvania, providing employees and their families with quality housing, education, and healthcare. In 1909, he and his wife established the Hershey Industrial School, now known as the Milton Hershey School, to offer education and care for orphaned boys. This commitment to community welfare reflects a model of corporate responsibility that aligns with modern principles of investing in the well-being of the workforce to achieve sustainable economic success.[5-7]

George W. Vanderbilt's vision for the Biltmore Estate in Asheville, North Carolina, extended beyond architectural grandeur to encompass environmental stewardship, agricultural innovation, and community investment. Collaborating with landscape architect Frederick Law Olmsted, Vanderbilt implemented the nation's first scientific forestry program, laying the groundwork for modern sustainable land management. He also founded Biltmore Farms in 1897, introducing advanced agricultural techniques and fostering a self-sustaining enterprise that supported local families.

Additionally, Vanderbilt developed Biltmore Village, providing housing, education, and healthcare for estate workers and their families. This holistic approach to community well-being reflected his commitment to responsible development, mirroring contemporary efforts to balance progress with sustainability. His legacy continues through Biltmore's ongoing conservation and sustainability initiatives.[8-10]

A Legacy of Pragmatism and Unity

While industrial pioneers like Henry Ford, Milton Hershey, and the Vanderbilt family are often celebrated for harnessing collective power to drive economic growth and public benefit, their legacies are far from spotless. Ford, for instance, espoused deeply antisemitic views and enforced racially segregated practices that ran counter to the very ideals of inclusive progress. Their stories underscore a broader truth: great wealth can be wielded to uplift society or to entrench personal power. Today, we see this tension echoed in figures like Elon Musk, Jeff Bezos, and Mark Zuckerberg—whose ventures often prioritize market dominance—versus philanthropists like Melinda and Bill Gates, Warren Buffett, and Mark Cuban, who have directed substantial resources toward public good.

When viewed in a historical context, my beliefs reflect the best traditions of American leadership—traditions that emphasize innovation, fairness, and the balance of individual rights with the collective good. These principles were neither purely liberal nor conservative; they were pragmatic. They recognized that progress requires both vision and compromise, that equality and opportunity are interdependent, and that innovation is meaningless without infrastructure to support it.

The challenge we face today is not a lack of innovative ideas but a lack of willingness to recognize their shared roots. As Barry Goldwater, Mitch McConnell (in his early career), and Abraham Lincoln demonstrated, the values of progress, fairness, and responsibility transcend party labels. They are the enduring principles upon which America's greatest successes have been built.

The Path Forward

It is time to reclaim this tradition of pragmatic leadership and shared responsibility. My beliefs are not a departure from history but a continuation of it. They are a call to honor the legacies of those who understood that the future of this nation depends not on ideological purity but on the ability to unite around common goals and shared values. As Lincoln once said, "The best way to predict the future is to create it." Together, we can create a future that honors the past while building a better tomorrow.

"I am convinced that most Americans now want to reverse the trend (of partisan politics). I think that concern for our vanishing freedoms is genuine. I think that the people's uneasiness in the stifling omnipresence of government has turned into something approaching alarm. But bemoaning the evil will not drive it back."—Barry Goldwater[11]

"THAT GOVERNMENT OF
THE PEOPLE,
BY THE PEOPLE,
FOR THE PEOPLE,
SHALL NOT PERISH FROM
THE EARTH."
ABRAHAM LINCOLN

For the PEOPLE

"Without liberty, law loses its nature and its name, and becomes oppression. Without law, liberty also loses its nature and its name, and becomes licentiousness."
—JAMES WILSON, FOUNDING FATHER

Balancing Order and Liberty

Government is both a protector and a threat to liberty; that dual nature of government is a constant in the human political experience. The framers of the Constitution aimed to thread that paradox through a system of checks and balances to enable a government that would serve and protect the governed. Indeed, this duality demands a careful calibration between empowerment and restraint—one that sits at the front and center of constitutional governance.

Today, the dual nature of government is clearer than ever. Technological innovation, worldwide interdependence, and complex financial systems have broadened the realm of governable activity in ways that the framers could hardly have imagined. From tools of surveillance to tools of regulatory oversight, the instruments of modern governments can be used for great good or great evil.

For instance, solving global problems like climate change, public health crises, and economic inequality requires effective government action. These efforts need coordinated action and, in many cases, strong intervention. These powers must be exercised with transparency, accountability, and a commitment to the public good, though. Without these constraints, even well-intentioned policies can have unintended consequences or lead to abuses of power.

The decline of government's ability to act—whether it be because of partisan gridlock, judicial overreach, or regulatory dismantlement—carries its own dangers. A government that cannot execute its basic functions due to weakness or dysfunction can leave society susceptible to outside threats, internal disorder, and economic turmoil.

Solutions are simple; it is politics that complicates matters.

Preserving the Balance

Government is essential in so many ways: to keeping our society in order, to maintaining justice, and to creating the conditions in which people and communities can flourish. Society would fall into chaos with no central authority to link the different layers of society and enforce laws, protect rights, and provide basic services. As Hobbes writes in *Leviathan*, without government, life would be "solitary, poor, nasty, brutish, and short."[12]

But the same powers that enable governments to secure liberty and stability also render them vulnerable to overreach. These powers, unimpeded, can transform into engines of oppression, as history has shown repeatedly. It was this built-in tension that the framers of the U.S. Constitution set out to answer.

The Constitution's framers, drawing on firsthand experience of British colonial authority and political philosophy, understood the risks posed by unrefereed authority. They crafted a system in which power was shared between three branches of government—legislative, executive, and judicial—to prevent any single entity from dominating the republic. Moreover, federalism dispersed power geographically, ensuring national policies were checked by state-level interests, and national representatives saw themselves answerable not just to their party but to multiple and diverse regions.

James Madison articulated the principle behind this design in "Federalist No. 51," stating that "ambition must be made to counteract ambition."[13] This principle highlights the framers' understanding that human nature, defined by self-interest and fallibility, requires institutional checks and balances. The Constitution sought to prevent any one individual or group from acquiring the power to challenge the Constitution by creating a system through which each of the branches and levels of government could check the others, maintaining a distributed and balanced power structure.

The Cost of Concentrated Power

History is replete with examples showing that concentrated power is freedom's greatest foe. Monarchies, oligarchies, and authoritarian regimes show that unchecked authority inevitably leads to corruption and the violation of the freedom of the individual. Power corrupts, as Lord Acton observed—*"Power tends to corrupt, and absolute power corrupts absolutely"*[14] —and that aphorism is just as true now as when it was first spoken in 1887. The framers of the United States Constitution knew this well, writing a system of checks and balances into our framework with the idea that no one entity should ever be allowed to control the republic. But history also teaches us that liberty requires vigilance; it is not self-generating.

The concentration of power within political elites can create a de facto oligarchy, even under the guise of democratic institutions. When lobbyists, special interest groups, or corporations exert disproportionate influence over legislation, the government risks prioritizing private interests over public welfare. Similarly, when elected officials prioritize personal gain, partisan advantage, or ideological purity over their constitutional responsibilities, the system falters.

In these scenarios, the safeguards envisioned by the framers—checks and balances, the rule of law, and accountability—are rendered ineffective, allowing power to accumulate in ways that undermine the very freedoms the government exists to protect.

Corporate Influence and Economic Concentration

The concentration of economic power is a direct threat to accountability—and to the notion that capitalism serves the people. Corporations like Tesla, Amazon, ExxonMobil, and major pharmaceutical giants exploit legal loopholes, influence policy, and manipulate markets to protect their dominance and profits. A 2023 report from the Institute on Taxation and Economic Policy found that 55 of the largest U.S. corporations paid zero federal income taxes in recent years—despite collectively earning over $40 billion in profits.[15,16] Armed with vast legal and lobbying resources, they dodge taxes, suppress competition, and extract wealth from public systems. This toxic fusion of private capital and political influence corrodes both democracy and capitalism, turning systems meant to promote innovation and public welfare into mechanisms of control and inequality.

And Americans enjoy core elements of democratic governance: regular elections, free speech, freedom of association, and the albeit still challenged right to vote. But these democratic values are at risk when powerful business organizations and a small, wealthy elite control policymaking. When the interests of the few always trump the needs of the many, America's contention that it is a truly democratic society is put in grave jeopardy.

Economic power is concentrated dangerously so that corporations exert power that at times matches or exceeds that of governments.

Mega corporations use their wealth to advocate for friendly policy, avoid taxes, and suppress competition. Such practices serve to exacerbate inequality, concentrating power within an elite minority, and leaving the wider population devoid of power. In these regulatory capture situations, industries wrest control of the agencies assigned to keep them in check, resulting in deprived areas like the environment, healthcare, and finance, focusing on profit instead of the public good.

This nefarious unification of political and economic power is reminiscent of objections against the British Crown in the colonial era, where laws were made to enclose the wealth of colonies for the use of the Crown and its associates at the cost of colonies' wealth and liberty. More broadly, our contemporary institutions have become entities more apt to reflect elite priorities than common welfare, to the detriment of everyday Americans forced to bear the consequences of policy designed for the rich. If they are not nipped in the bud, this dynamic threatens to further undermine the democratic principles on which the United States was built.

"The USA is a Plutocratic Oligarchy controlled by a wealthy and influential few." This was according to a study by Princeton University professor Martin Gilens and Northwestern University professor Benjamin Page.

The two professors found that the wealthy few drive policy, while the average American wields little power. The two professors reached this conclusion after analyzing responses to 1,779 survey questions posed from 1981 to 2002 about public policy issues. They disaggregated the responses by income level, then calculated how frequently certain income levels and organized interest groups got what they wanted in terms of policy.[17]

"American democracy is a sham, no matter how much it is pumped by the oligarchs who run the country (and who run the nation's 'news' media," writes Eric Zuess on the website CounterPunch. "In other words, the US is like Russia or most of the other sketchy 'electoral' 'democratic' countries. We weren't before but we are clearly now."[18]

A System Undermined by Wealth and Influence

The framers of the Constitution sought to guard against tyranny, spreading power across branches and levels of government to counter ambition with ambition. But such protections are today routinely circumvented or ignored. Think about the systemic effects of the *Citizens United v. Federal Election Commission* U.S. Supreme Court ruling (2010), which treated money as equivalent to speech and led to a flood of corporate and individual contributions in politics. This decision has transformed elections into contests with the richest and most powerful, at the expense of the voices of everyday citizens, and eroding trust in representative democracy.[19]

Even the judiciary, ordinarily regarded as the bulwark for constitutional integrity, has not been immune to accountability erosion. Amid the recent controversies surrounding undisclosed gifts, financial entanglements, and perceived partisan loyalties among Supreme Court justices, public trust in this central branch of government has eroded further. When the independence of the judiciary is in question, the entire system of checks and balances fails.

In the meantime, Congress has surrendered much of its legislative authority to special interests. Instead of laws that align with the needs and wants of the population, we see legislation written by lobbyists and corporate donors. Regulatory bodies, designed to safeguard the public good, frivolously become beholden to "revolving door" placements, when former insiders become the arbiters of the industries from which they drew their previous income.

The Danger of Polarization

"United we stand, divided we fall" is not just a well-used piece of advice; it is also a deep warning about what division brings. At times of extreme polarization throughout American history, the nation's resilience has been tested. From the Revolutionary War to the Civil War to the cultural revolution of the '60s, internal conflict threatened to tear apart the fabric of the republic. Although these events made the country stronger through hard-earned lessons, they are also solemn reminders of the price of division.

The Civil War—the single most devastating example of polarization in U.S. history—helps make clear the danger of not addressing ideological and moral divides early before they spiral out of control. The war was the result of decades of unaddressed tensions surrounding slavery, states' rights, and economic disparity—tensions that might have been alleviated had leaders and citizens approached issues with more adaptability, with a desire to realize the founding ideals of liberty, equality, and justice.

Polarization Today

It is an era in which the political, cultural, and ideological divisions have deepened to a point reminiscent of those darker days. Partisan rhetoric, social media echo chambers, and the gradual erosion of trust in institutions have widened divides to such an extent that finding common ground often seems unattainable.

This polarization exists not only in Washington, D.C.; it trickles down into communities, workplaces, and even families. Political parties have become a part of the identities of individuals and create an "us and them" mentality that calls into question your willingness to talk or collaborate with people outside the party line. The result is a perilous atmosphere in which dissent too easily turns to enmity, and where solutions to urgent challenges—like climate change, healthcare, and social equity—are postponed or blocked.

The Risks of Continued Polarization

Unchecked political polarization poses a significant threat to the stability of democratic governance. When political rivals are viewed as enemies rather than co-governors, the willingness to compromise diminishes, leading to legislative gridlock and undermining democratic institutions. This environment fosters extremism and paves the way for authoritarian tendencies. Studies have shown that severe polarization can erode social cohesion, disrupt political stability, and increase the likelihood of democratic erosion.[20]

Additionally, as polarization intensifies, citizens may become more willing to trade off democratic principles for partisan interests, further endangering the democratic process.21

Unchecked polarization is a danger to the stability of democratic governance itself. When political rivals become adversaries instead of co-governors, willingness to compromise diminishes. It leads to gridlock, undermines institutions, and paves the way for extremism and authoritarianism.

Such divisions have historically produced unrest, instability, and, in severe cases, civil war. Today, we see signals of this danger:

> **Erosion of Institutional Trust:** Trust in government, media, and even science has tumbled dramatically, leaving a vacuum of reliable authority.

> **Rising extremism:** Torch-carrying, name-serving fringe movements that reject democracy and plurality in favor of groupthink are gaining force under polarization.

> **Decline of Open Discourse:** Partisan polarization ensures no meaningful action on the major problems facing the country, leaving problems to fester and grow.

Learning from History

History offers valuable lessons about the dangers of polarization and the paths to reconciliation. The aftermath of the Civil War, for instance, illustrates both the challenges and opportunities of rebuilding unity. The period of Reconstruction demonstrated the necessity of addressing systemic injustices while also revealing the perils of failing to sustain those efforts. The Civil Rights Movement of the twentieth century similarly showed the power of nonviolent action and moral leadership in overcoming deep societal divides.

These moments remind us that progress is possible when leaders and citizens alike commit to principles of justice, equity, and dialogue. They also underscore the importance of addressing the root causes of division—whether economic inequality, social injustice, or political corruption—before they reach a breaking point.

Parallels with the Present

Today's polarization mirrors past crises in several significant ways. Economic disparities, much like those that existed between industrial and agrarian states leading up to the Civil War, are a major factor contributing to the deepening divides in modern society. The widening wealth gap today has created a divide that is not only economic but also social, reinforcing divisions and hindering social mobility. Similarly, cultural clashes are becoming more pronounced, with competing visions of America—whether rural versus urban, or traditional versus progressive—creating ideological and cultural rifts akin to those seen in previous eras. These divisions are fueling tensions that often seem insurmountable, yet they echo struggles faced by earlier generations.

Political dysfunction also reflects a breakdown in the collaborative spirit that was central to the founding of the United States. The inability of Congress and other institutions to effectively address pressing national issues today is a stark contrast to the ideals envisioned by the framers of the Constitution. This dysfunction undermines public trust in the political process and exacerbates the sense of division across the country.

However, there is hope for overcoming these challenges. The same principles that guided America through past trials—compromise, accountability, and a deep commitment to shared ideals—remain relevant today. These enduring values can serve as a foundation for addressing the current divisions, offering a path toward reconciliation and progress. By embracing these principles, the nation can find ways to bridge its divides and work toward a more united future.

The Erosion of Accountability

The parallels between the grievances of the American colonies and the dysfunctions of modern governance serve as a sobering reminder of how systems, even those designed to prevent tyranny, can decay over time. When the colonies rebelled against the British monarchy, they were pushing back against a system that prioritized the interests of the elite—lords, landowners, and foreign powers—over the common good of the people. This system, which excluded many from political participation and denied them fair representation, eventually triggered a revolt.

Today, we face a similarly entrenched dynamic, albeit under the guise of a democratic framework. Despite the outward appearance of a government of the people, modern systems often reflect the influence of powerful elites, corporations, and special interest groups that hold sway over policy decisions, leaving many ordinary citizens feeling sidelined. Just as the colonists found themselves voiceless in the decisions that affected their lives, many today experience a similar sense of powerlessness in the face of a political system that seems increasingly dominated by the interests of the few. This troubling parallel raises the question of how effectively our democratic institutions can respond to the needs and rights of the broader population when the very framework of governance is eroding.

The Path to Civil Unrest

Unchecked, these trends risk pushing the nation toward greater polarization and even civil unrest. When citizens feel alienated from their government and believe the system is rigged against them, they lose faith in democratic processes. This alienation breeds anger, division, and, in extreme cases, violence. The symptoms of this erosion are already evident. There is a growing sense of voter apathy and widespread disillusionment with politics, as many Americans feel disconnected from the political establishment and believe their voices no longer matter. This discontent has fueled the rise of populist movements driven by anti-establishment sentiment, further deepening societal divides. At the same time, the country has become more polarized, with communities fracturing along ideological, cultural, and political lines, undermining the sense of national unity that once held the nation together. These trends threaten the fabric of our nation, and if left unchecked, could erode the foundations of democracy itself.

A Legislative Process Distorted by Special Interests

The legislative process in Congress has increasingly been compromised by the influence of special interests, leading to the inclusion of "pork barrel" spending and non-germane amendments that cater to specific groups rather than the broader public. For instance, the 2013 fiscal cliff deal included an estimated $70 million in tax credits benefiting NASCAR tracks, illustrating how legislation can be tailored to favor particular industries.[22]

Moreover, the involvement of lobbyists in drafting legislation further skews the lawmaking process toward corporate interests. A

2014 investigation revealed that lobbyists played a significant role in crafting a banking deregulation bill, with Senator Elizabeth Warren highlighting that such legislation posed risks to the economy by favoring large financial institutions.[23]

These practices not only undermine the integrity of democratic governance but also perpetuate inequality, as policies are shaped to benefit the influential few over the general populace.

The Judiciary and the Decline of Trust

The judiciary, especially the Supreme Court, was designed to be an impartial arbiter of constitutional principles. However, recent revelations about financial gifts and undisclosed relationships between justices and powerful interests have tarnished its reputation.[24] When judicial decisions are perceived as being influenced by external factors, the integrity of the entire legal system is called into question.

The 2010 Supreme Court decision in *Citizens United v. Federal Election Commission* significantly altered the landscape of American political campaigns by equating monetary expenditures with free speech under the First Amendment. This ruling effectively allowed corporations and wealthy individuals to spend unlimited amounts on independent political activities, thereby amplifying their influence over elections. As a result, political campaigns have evolved into billion-dollar enterprises, where success often hinges on fundraising capabilities rather than the merit of ideas. For instance, the 2024 U.S. presidential election saw combined fundraising efforts of approximately $2.5 billion between the major candidates, underscoring the escalating financial arms race in modern politics.[25]

The result? A political environment where the voices of ordinary Americans are drowned out by those with the deepest pockets.

A Government Failing Its Founding Principles

The dangers of concentrated power were clear to the Constitution's framers. By creating a system of checks and balances, they intended to diffuse power and protect against tyranny. But they knew these mechanisms would work only if the people remained vigilant in their oversight. James Madison wisely cautioned, "A dependence on the people is, no doubt, the primary control on the government; but experience has taught mankind the necessity of auxiliary precautions."[13]

The increasing reliance on executive orders (EOs) by U.S. presidents has raised concerns about the overreach of executive authority, potentially undermining the legislative process and contributing to partisan gridlock. Examining the trend from President Ronald Reagan through President Joe Biden illustrates this shift:[26–29]

- **Ronald Reagan (1981–1989):** Issued 381 executive orders over eight years, averaging approximately 47.6 per year.

- **George H.W. Bush (1989–1993):** Signed 166 executive orders during his single term, averaging 41.5 annually.

- **Bill Clinton (1993–2001):** Issued 364 executive orders across two terms, with an average of 45.5 per year.

- **George W. Bush (2001–2009):** Signed 291 executive orders over eight years, averaging 36.4 annually.

- **Barack Obama (2009–2017):** Issued 276 executive orders during his presidency, averaging 34.5 per year.

- **Donald Trump (2017–2025):** Signed 220 executive orders in his first term, averaging 55 per year. As of March 22, 2025, during his second term's first 100 days has issued 98 executive orders.

- **Joe Biden (2021–2025):** Issued 162 executive orders during his single term, averaging 40.5 annually.

This pattern highlights a sustained use of executive orders to implement policy, especially during periods of legislative gridlock. While executive orders are legitimate instruments for managing federal operations, their increased deployment can blur the separation of powers, allowing presidents to bypass Congress and centralize authority. This trend underscores the challenges posed by partisan divisions and raises questions about the balance of power within the U.S. government.

It is not that the system fails because the framework in place is intrinsically flawed; the system has failed because those who are supposed to uphold the framework—the elected, the justices, the citizenry—have neglected their duties. A failure to fulfill those responsibilities undermines the balance of power and indeed threatens the very stability of democratic governance itself.

The Role of Citizens: Eternal Vigilance

The future of our republic hinges on our collective ability to reimagine accountability and renew our dedication to the ideals of liberty, equality, and justice. The urgent question is whether we possess the courage and determination to rise to this challenge.

Benjamin Franklin's famous quip—"A Republic, if you can keep it"[30]—reminds us that maintaining a republic is not a passive endeavor. It requires active participation, vigilance, and a steadfast commitment to safeguarding the principles upon which our nation was founded. Although eroding accountability is a huge problem, it can also be reversed. History tells us that when people across this country organize with a purpose, change for the better becomes possible.

The framers of the Constitution recognized that structural safeguards alone would never be enough. The greatest systems in the world still rely on the virtue, attention, and participation of their citizens. James Madison wisely noted that government exists not because men are angels, but because they are not. Recognizing this inherent imperfection, the framers designed a system of checks and balances, trusting future generations to preserve and refine it.

But no matter how well-designed a system may be, it can implode in the hands of public servants who put their self-interest ahead of their public service. It is the people's responsibility to ensure that government, as our Founding Fathers envisioned, is a force for good, a protector of liberty and justice. Each generation must meet the challenge of maintaining that delicate balance of liberty and order envisioned by the framers.

As John Philpot Curran observed, "The price of liberty is eternal vigilance."[31] But this vigilance must extend beyond passive observation. It demands active engagement in the democratic process, informed advocacy, and a resolute commitment to holding leaders accountable. Citizens must resist the urge to view government as inherently virtuous or irredeemably corrupt. Instead, it should be seen as a powerful and essential tool—one that, like any tool, must be wielded with care and responsibility.

To fulfill this duty, we must, collectively, advocate for policies that sustain and strengthen democratic values, support leaders who demonstrate integrity and vision, and remain ever-alert to the dangers of unchecked power. This is not an easy task, especially in a polarized and divided political landscape, but it is a necessary one. Our collective vigilance, integrity, and dedication to principle will determine whether the ideals of liberty and justice will endure for future generations.

For the VOTER

**"The government is the strongest of which
every man feels himself a part."**

— THOMAS JEFFERSON

The Fifteenth Amendment

The right to vote is basic to American democracy, guaranteed by the Constitution, and extended over the years to make the system more inclusive and fair. The Fifteenth Amendment specifically forbids discrimination against voters based on race, color, or history of servitude. But this right remains undermined by systemic disenfranchisement, innuendo campaign finance, restrictive voting laws, gerrymandering, and misinformation.

Disenfranchisement of Certain Populations

The New Deal, Dean Acheson wrote approvingly in *A Democrat Looks at His Party,* "conceived of the federal government as the whole people organized to do what had to be done."[32] A year later, Mr. Larson, in *A Republican Looks at His Party,* echoed a similar sentiment about the role of government. He described the "underlying philosophy" of Modern Republicanism as the belief that "if a job has to be done to meet the needs of the people, and no one else can do it, then it is the proper function of the federal government."[33]

While Democrats and Republicans often differ in their policy approaches and ideological rhetoric, both parties have historically shared a core belief in the role of government as a necessary instrument for addressing societal challenges. However, the growing chasm between their platforms—and the increasingly extreme rhetoric from prominent figures on both sides—has fueled polarization and disillusionment among voters. As a result, many Americans feel alienated from the political process: over 40% of registered voters believe their vote doesn't matter or won't make a difference. Even more telling, a majority—51%—now identify as Independents, signaling a broad rejection of the two-party system. This growing bloc of unaffiliated voters reflects deep dissatisfaction with partisan politics and a desire for more representative, pragmatic, and solutions-focused governance.

A Path Forward: Rebuilding Faith in Democracy

Restoring trust in America's electoral system requires an unwavering commitment to fairness, transparency, and inclusivity. Equal access to voting for all citizens must be safeguarded to ensure that no one is disenfranchised due to systemic barriers or deliberate suppression. Legislative and presidential elections should reflect fair representation, with reforms addressing gerrymandering and outdated electoral practices that distort the will of the people. Reducing the undue influence of wealth and special interests is essential to reinvigorate public confidence, ensuring that policy decisions are driven by the collective good rather than the power of money.

Making these changes demands bipartisan cooperation and persistent public advocacy. A renewed dedication to the ideals of equity, representation, and accountability can leave America's democracy stronger. If Congress can confront these challenges with brave and principled action, the nation can reaffirm its commitment to the right of every vote to count and the electoral system serving all citizens with integrity.

Restore Voter Integrity

Providing measures we can count on—accessibility to the system and security and confidence in the electoral process—are a balm to this national wound. A verified voter ID system can provide a check that protects our elections while maintaining the most basic right we have, to vote. Requiring government-issued photo IDs to vote at the polls is vital in addressing the concerns of fraud while protecting fair and inclusive access to democracy. But any such system must ensure against disenfranchisement by providing free voter IDs to all eligible citizens. Utilizing existing infrastructure like that used by the US passport system, managed by the US Postal Service (USPS), could help make this happen. When citizens register to vote, they could apply for free voter identification, which would be sent to them by mail once their identity is verified to ensure no financial or logistical barriers prevent them from voting.

With a voter ID system, individuals would be less likely to question election integrity, due to the additional layer of verification bolstering their trust in the electoral process. Voter fraud is so rare that it happens only in handfuls[34,35]—studies indicate rates as low as 0.0000845% in states like Arizona[34, 35]—but this would address perceptions of the system's vulnerability. IDs should be free and available to the public through trusted providers such as the USPS and the state agencies; mobile units and outreach teams should offer services to those who may not have access, including people in rural areas, the elderly, and those in low-income communities. This widespread access would guarantee that no voter gets disenfranchised because they lack appropriate identification or live too far from an enrollment center.

A standardized voter ID system would also ease administrative burdens on Election Day. A single accepted form of ID for everyone would speed up check-in at polling places and reduce confusion. The institution of voter IDs can be combined with robust fraud prevention systems, secure databases, and real-time verification that guarantees that legitimate citizens cast votes. These reforms should come alongside public education campaigns to combat myths, build confidence, and explain the goals and implementation of voter ID initiatives.

Such an endeavor must also be part of a larger effort to promote electoral transparency and access. Transparent auditing, a ban on gerrymandering, and equal access to polling places are necessary to make elections fair. Overcoming such challenges with a holistic approach can reinforce U.S. dedication to democratic systems that empower every citizen's voice to be heard, honored, and protected.

Remove Voting Constraints

One of the most significant barriers to voting in the United States is a lack of opportunity, particularly for hourly and shift workers whose rigid schedules make it difficult to access the polls. This challenge disproportionately affects low-income individuals and marginalized communities, leading to inequities in voter turnout and undermining the principle of equal participation in democracy.

A simple yet transformative solution is to designate Election Day as a federal holiday by shifting Presidents' Day to the first Tuesday in November. This change would remove financial and professional obstacles, ensuring that workers do not have to choose between earning a paycheck and exercising their right to vote. Repurposing an existing holiday rather than creating a new one would maintain a balance between civic engagement and workplace productivity, making it a practical and impactful reform.

There is historical evidence that shows that removing logistical barriers to voting, whether through early voting or expanded hours, increases voter turnout. A dedicated holiday would further improve accessibility, especially for communities that encounter systemic barriers to voting. Also, staggering work hours means less congestion at polling places, shorter lines, and a more efficient process. Taking this step would make the process better for all voters and lead to greater participation by a wider demographic.

Making Election Day a federal holiday would also be a strong reaffirmation of the nation's democratic values. The increased emphasis that such a day would provide would make a clear statement about the role civic engagement plays in American society by elevating voting to the status of a national holiday. It embodies a shared dedication to making certain that every voice is heard and every vote matters.

Moreover, this with other voting accessibility measures, including expansion of early voting and mail-in ballot options, creates an overall voting system more representative of the people. Meeting the unique challenges of hourly workers is an important part of reducing disparities in the electoral process and ensuring that all Americans, regardless of their financial circumstances, can fully engage in shaping the country's future.

Universal Voter Access

Access to the ballot box is fundamental to a functioning democracy, yet significant barriers persist, particularly in underserved and marginalized communities. Ensuring universal voter access requires addressing systemic challenges to create a fair, equitable, and efficient electoral system.

Equipping Polling Stations: Polling stations must be adequately staffed and equipped to handle the needs of voters. This includes providing sufficient voting machines, trained personnel, and accommodations for individuals with disabilities. Underserved areas, particularly rural regions, and densely populated urban centers often experience long lines and logistical issues that deter voter participation. Investing in these areas ensures that no voters are left behind due to inadequate resources.

Expanding Early Voting: Early voting provides flexibility for individuals who may face scheduling conflicts on Election Day. By offering extended periods for casting ballots, voters gain more opportunities to participate without the stress of navigating busy polling stations. States that have implemented robust early voting programs report higher turnout and reduced strain on Election Day infrastructure.

Enhancing Mail-In Ballot Access: Mail-in voting has proven to be a reliable and secure method for increasing voter participation. By allowing voters to complete their ballots at their convenience, this option eliminates the need for travel to polling locations and accommodates those with mobility issues, caregiving responsibilities, or other barriers. Ensuring that all voters can easily request and return mail-in ballots is essential for broadening access.

Federal Voting Holiday: Establishing a federal holiday for Election Day emphasizes the importance of voting and removes a significant constraint for hourly workers and those with rigid schedules. Coupled with expanded voting options, a federal holiday ensures that all citizens have the time and flexibility to exercise their right to vote without facing undue hardship.

Technology and Accessibility Improvements: Across the United States, efforts to modernize election systems are unfolding at an uneven pace—marked by significant progress in some states, persistent challenges in others, and growing debate over what modernization should look like.

In **Pennsylvania**, officials are replacing a 20-year-old voter registration system with a modern platform known as **Civix**, designed to streamline voter data management, campaign finance filings, and election night reporting. The $10 million system is expected to be fully functional by the 2028 presidential election, improving transparency and efficiency across the board.[36]

Meanwhile, **Connecticut** is considering adopting **Ranked Choice Voting (RCV)**, which allows voters to rank candidates by preference. Advocates argue that this approach encourages civil discourse and ensures that winning candidates reflect broader public support— potentially increasing voter engagement and reducing polarization.[37]

Not all modernization efforts have expanded access. In **New Hampshire**, new voter registration laws now require proof of U.S. citizenship. While intended to prevent fraud, the policy has already excluded some eligible voters, sparking concern among voting rights advocates who warn that such measures risk suppressing participation from underrepresented communities.[38]

Legal and political barriers have also stalled modernization efforts in other states. In **Michigan**, Republican lawmakers have asked the U.S. Supreme Court to strike down parts of a voter-approved election reform law, claiming it infringes on the legislature's constitutional authority to set election procedures.[39] Similarly, in **Georgia**, the state's Supreme Court is reviewing whether the State Election Board exceeded its authority in implementing new election rules—highlighting the tension between election agencies and lawmakers.[40]

Even when technology is implemented, it brings new challenges. Election officials in swing states are preparing for misinformation campaigns, cyber threats, and voter intimidation fueled by conspiracy theories about voting machines and ballot tampering. The ongoing threat of disinformation looms large, undermining the very confidence that modernization aims to restore.[41]

Despite these roadblocks, technology continues to open doors for many voters. Online voter registration, ballot tracking systems, and accessible voting equipment for people with disabilities are being adopted in various jurisdictions to help ensure that **every voter can participate with dignity and confidence.** For example, in **Texas**, counties like Bexar have implemented curbside voting equipped with intercom systems, and polling locations now offer ASL interpreter services via video to better serve deaf and hard-of-hearing voters.[42]

These advancements reflect the potential of modernization—but also its complexity. True progress requires more than new tools. It demands a thoughtful balance between access and security, clear legal frameworks, adequate funding, and above all, a commitment to public trust.

Targeting Underserved Communities: Special attention must be given to communities that have historically faced systemic barriers to voting—particularly low-income neighborhoods, communities of color, and rural populations. Ensuring equal access to the ballot goes beyond simply placing polling locations in these areas; it requires sustained outreach, civic education, language access, and the provision of resources that empower voters to participate fully and confidently in the democratic process.

Yet this mission becomes significantly more difficult in states where elected officials—often under Republican leadership—have enacted laws or policies that restrict voting access. These include purging voter rolls, limiting early voting, closing polling locations in minority neighborhoods, imposing strict voter ID laws, and reducing access to mail-in voting. In such environments, the challenge isn't just logistical—it's deeply political.

Even when the state apparatus works against them, underserved communities can still be reached and empowered—through a combination of legal defense, civic education, on-the-ground mobilization, and digital innovation. While the barriers are real, they are not insurmountable. The fight for voting rights has always required perseverance, strategy, and community—and those tools are still available today.

Restoring Fair Representation

Gerrymandering—the deliberate manipulation of electoral district boundaries to favor a particular political party—undermines the democratic principle of fair representation. By creating "safe" districts, gerrymandering disenfranchises voters, reduces competitive elections, and exacerbates polarization.

Defenders of gerrymandering often justify the practice by arguing that it reflects natural demographic clustering, suggesting that politically homogeneous districts are an inevitable outcome of populations choosing to live among like-minded individuals. Others claim that drawing safe districts enhances community representation by keeping cultural or geographic communities intact.

Politicians from both major parties have, at times, openly acknowledged and defended partisan gerrymandering. For instance, during a 2016 redistricting hearing, North Carolina Republican Representative David Lewis stated:

"I propose that we draw the maps to give a partisan advantage to 10 Republicans and three Democrats because I do not believe it's possible to draw a map with 11 Republicans and two Democrats."[43]

Similarly, former Maryland Governor Martin O'Malley, a Democrat, admitted in a 2019 deposition that the intent behind Maryland's 2011 redistricting was to favor his party:

"It was my intent to create...a district where the people would be more likely to elect a Democrat than a Republican."[44]

These candid admissions reveal a bipartisan willingness to engage in gerrymandering for political gain, often justified by the belief that achieving partisan objectives through redistricting is a legitimate exercise of political power. However, such practices raise significant ethical and democratic concerns, as they can entrench incumbents, diminish electoral competitiveness, and undermine public confidence in the electoral process.

Addressing gerrymandering requires a commitment to fair representation and the establishment of impartial redistricting processes that prioritize the interests of voters over partisan advantage.

To address gerrymandering, we must establish independent, nonpartisan commissions to draw electoral districts. States like California and Michigan have successfully implemented these reforms, ensuring fair representation. Mandate that districts be drawn based on population size and geographical contiguity without considering partisan data. Ensure polling places are capable of processing 100 percent of (potential) votes cast during each polling location's open hours (typically eight hours). Empower courts to assess and strike down unfairly drawn districts.

By addressing these critical areas, **_universal voter access_** can transform the electoral process into one that truly reflects the will of the people. With comprehensive reforms, America can take significant strides toward a more inclusive and participatory democracy, ensuring that every voice is heard and every vote counts. We must restore voter confidence that their vote COUNTS.

Campaign Finance Reform

In modern America, the concentration of political power in the hands of wealthy donors and corporations is overshadowing the influence of ordinary citizens. The Supreme Court's decision in _Citizens United v. Federal Election Commission (2010)_, under the guise of free speech, allowed unlimited political spending by corporations and special interest groups, equating monetary contributions with "free speech." The ruling gave undue influence to the wealthy elite while diminishing the voice of everyday citizens. This ruling exacerbated the longstanding issue of corporate oligarchy, where financial power is used to shape policy and legislation, often at the expense of the public good.

Citizens United has been a subject of extensive debate among constitutional scholars, many of whom contend that the ruling is fundamentally flawed and undermines democratic principles.

Laurence H. Tribe, a prominent constitutional law professor at Harvard University, has criticized the decision for equating corporate entities with individuals in the context of political speech. He argues that this perspective "obscures the very real injustice and distortion entailed in the phenomenon of some people using other people's money to support candidates they have made no decision to support, or to oppose candidates they have made no decision to oppose."[45]

Similarly, **Zephyr Teachout,** a legal scholar specializing in corruption and constitutional law, has highlighted the detrimental impact of **Citizens United** on the integrity of the political system. In her work, she emphasizes how the ruling facilitates an influx of money in politics, potentially leading to corruption and a departure from democratic ideals.[46,47]

Furthermore, a study conducted by the University of Maryland's Program for Public Consultation found that a significant majority of Americans—across the political spectrum—support a constitutional amendment to overturn **Citizens United,** reflecting widespread public concern over the decision's implications.[48]

These perspectives underscore a broader discourse within the legal community and the general public, questioning the constitutional validity of **Citizens United** and advocating for reforms to mitigate its impact on the democratic process.

Citizens United has provided a mechanism for veiled campaign contributions by foreign entities. We must restrain pressure groups from seeking special privilege favors at the expense of the general public.[19] It is imperative that we make campaign contributions transparent. One way we exercise political freedom is to vote for the candidate of our choice. Another way is to use our money to try to persuade other voters to make a similar choice—that is, to contribute to our candidate's campaign. If either of these freedoms is violated, the consequences are very grave not only for the individual voter and contributor but for the society whose free political processes depend on a wide distribution of political power.

It is in the second of these areas, that of political contributions, that political action committees seriously compromise American freedom. They do this by spending the money of corporate, wealthy, and often foreign governments. It is impossible to say just how much is spent by these entities on political campaigns; certainly, one cannot tell from the amounts officially reported, which invariably present a grossly distorted picture.

PAC political activity is not confined, of course, to direct financial contributions. In fact, this is one of its smallest endeavors. PACs provide manpower for Election Day chores—for making phone calls, driving cars, manning the polls, and so on. Often, the people who perform these chores are reimbursed for their time off out of "political donations." PACs also sponsor social media and television programs and distribute a huge volume of printed material designed to support the candidate of the PAC's choice. In short, they perform all the functions of a regular party organization.

Now the evil here is twofold. For one thing, the PAC's decision whether to support candidate X or candidate Y—whether to help the Republican Party or the Democratic Party—is made by a handful of top donors. These few people are thus able to wield tremendous political power with the ability to spend other people's money.[49] No one else in America is so privileged.

All political contributions, whether from individuals, from corporations, or made through PACs and "dark money" organizations, should be fully disclosed. We should cap corporate contributions and prohibit foreign entities from contributing to U.S. elections. We should also implement publicly funded election models like those in Maine and Arizona, where candidates receive public funding in exchange for rejecting private donations, leveling the playing field for candidates without wealthy backers.

Election Influence in the Digital Age

Foreign states are advancing digital and physical means to repress individual critics and diaspora communities abroad and in the United States. Foreign states are also growing more sophisticated in digital influence operations that try to affect the U.S. public's views, sway voters' perspectives, shift policies, and create social and political upheaval.[50,51] Their impact has become evident on U.S. policies and undermining confidence in the U.S. electoral process. We must guard against digital authoritarianism and transnational repression.

Building Trust in the Electoral Process

Misinformation and foreign interference have deeply eroded public confidence in the integrity of U.S. elections. Never in U.S. history has voter fraud been proven to influence an election—local, state, or federal—especially for the POTUS.[35] While evidence shows voter fraud is exceedingly rare and cannot be eliminated in its entirety, persistent claims of election manipulation have sown doubt and division. We must counter this misinformation.

We must partner with social media platforms to detect and counteract false narratives while ensuring transparency in content moderation. We must launch campaigns to educate voters on the electoral process and counteract myths about election security. We must restore civics classes in public schools.

Ranked-Choice Voting: Reducing Polarization

Ranked-choice voting (RCV) provides a more sophisticated way to participate in elections, permitting us to rank candidates.[52] The Maine and Alaska systems already in existence allow voters to rank candidates in order of preference—a move that would decrease polarization and encourage coalition-building among candidates. Implementation should start with local and state pilot programs to build public familiarity and confidence in the system. The result is that candidates who win have real majority support, and vote-splitting and negative campaigning does not matter so much.

RCV is an electoral system that allows voters to rank candidates in order of preference—first choice, second choice, third, and so on. If no candidate receives a majority of first-choice votes, the candidate with the fewest votes is eliminated. Voters who chose the eliminated candidate have their votes reallocated to their next-highest remaining choice. This process repeats in rounds until one candidate receives a majority and is declared the winner.

RCV proponents argue that the system leads to more representative and inclusive elections by limiting the impact of vote-splitting and encouraging candidates to reach a wider electorate. It can reduce negative campaigning, because candidates are investing in being voters' second or third choices, if not their first. RCV is used in some U.S. cities and states and in countries like Australia and Ireland for some elections. But critics are concerned with its complexity and potential for voter confusion—especially in large or multi-candidate races. Still, many proponents view ranked choice voting as, though far from perfect, an important mechanism to help the bottom line of increased democratic participation and more civil political discourse.

The Electoral College: A Broken System

The history of electing the president of the United States via delegates originated in the Constitutional Convention of 1787, where the Founders strove to strike a balance between popular sovereignty and restraint against mob rule, and created the Electoral College.[53]

The way it works is that each state receives electors equal to the number of senators and representatives it has in Congress. Electors were originally selected by each state legislature rather than by its voters and were expected to exercise independent judgment in deciding on the presidency. This was driven by the tensions of limited national political infrastructure, slow information diffusion, and concerns over excessive populism.

Over the years, the function of the Electoral College has changed. By the mid-nineteenth century the political parties had started nominating both candidates and electors pledged to those candidates, thus bringing the electoral process more into line with the party. The well-established system of electing a president through the Electoral College—which was originally intended to balance the interests of populous and less populous states—has increasingly departed from the democratic ideal of "one person, one vote." Its winner-take-all method of assigning delegates in most states can result in situations in which the candidate who tallies the most popular votes across America can still end up losing the presidency, a scenario that has played out five times in American history (1824, 1876, 2000, and 2016). The electoral college over-represents smaller population states and swing states.[54-57] If a president wins, say, Florida by 50.1 percent to 49.9 percent, he or she garners all 30 electoral votes.

The Electoral College is anti-democratic. The District of Columbia and citizens in U.S. territories, including Puerto Rico and Guam, have no representation in the Electoral College. The Electoral College allocations must be reassessed.

Reforming the Electoral College is a critical step toward ensuring that the United States' electoral system better reflects the will of the people and promotes fair representation. One proposed reform is the proportional allocation of electoral votes, in which each state's electoral votes are distributed based on the percentage of the popular vote that each candidate receives. In the case of Florida, the winner of an extremely tight race would earn 16 of 30 votes. This approach would reduce the all-or-nothing stakes of swing states, giving more weight to votes cast in traditionally overlooked regions and ensuring a more equitable reflection of voter preferences.

Another proposal involves the National Popular Vote Interstate Compact, a cooperative agreement among states to pledge their electoral votes to the candidate who wins the national popular vote. This agreement would take effect once enough states join to constitute a majority of the Electoral College, effectively aligning the system with the popular vote without requiring a constitutional amendment.[58]

The most transformative reform would be to abolish the Electoral College altogether and adopt a direct popular vote for presidential elections. This change would ensure that every citizen's vote carries equal weight, regardless of geographic location, and eliminate the disproportionate influence of smaller or swing states. A direct popular vote system would make every voter's participation meaningful, fostering greater trust in the democratic process and reinforcing the principle of one person, one vote.

These reform efforts aim to address long-standing criticisms of the Electoral College, restore public confidence in the electoral system, and ensure that the government truly represents the will of the people. By prioritizing fairness, equity, and transparency, the United States can create an electoral process that reflects the diverse voices of its citizens and strengthens the foundation of its democracy.

For SECULAR GOVERNMENT

"Leave the matter of religion to the family altar, the church, and the private school, supported entirely by private contributions. Keep the church and state forever separate."
—ULYSSES S. GRANT

The Threat of Religious Control Over Public Policy

"Can any of us refute the wisdom of Madison and the other framers? Can anyone look at the carnage in Iran, the bloodshed in Northern Ireland or the bombs bursting in Lebanon and yet question the dangers of injecting religious issues into the affairs of state?"[11] —Barry Goldwater

The separation of church and state is not merely a legal principle; it is a moral and philosophical commitment to the ideals of democracy, pluralism, and individual liberty. This division ensures that no single ideology—religious or otherwise—dominates public policy, safeguards the rights of minorities, and fosters a governance system rooted in reason and shared values rather than divine mandates.

The warnings of Ulysses S. Grant and Barry Goldwater resonate across generations, illustrating the dangers of intertwining religion with politics. Their insights provide a framework for understanding why this separation is crucial and the risks posed by movements that seek to erode it.

History and contemporary events provide ample evidence that merging religion with governance undermines democratic principles, weakens individual freedoms, and often results in systemic oppression. When religious ideologies shape public policy, they tend to enforce exclusionary dogmas that marginalize minorities, deepen societal divisions, and foster authoritarian tendencies.

The Global Impact of Religious-Political Fusion

Religious control over governance has produced some of the most destructive and divisive conflicts in history, undermining peace and equality in diverse societies. A closer look at global examples highlights these dangers:

Northern Ireland: Sectarian Strife. For decades, Northern Ireland was torn apart by The Troubles (late 1960s to 1998)—a period marked by violent conflict between Catholic nationalists and Protestant unionists (Unionists believe that **Northern Ireland should remain part of the United Kingdom**). Political institutions, such as housing and voting rights, were heavily biased in favor of Protestants, marginalizing Catholics and fueling resentment. Over 3,500 people were killed and tens of thousands were injured in a struggle rooted in religious identity and political inequality. This conflict underscores how religious favoritism in governance erodes trust, stokes violence, and creates generational scars.[59]

Iran: Theocratic Oppression. Since the Islamic Revolution of 1979, Iran has operated under a theocratic regime where Sharia law dictates governance. Women face systemic discrimination, such as mandatory veiling and restrictions on employment, driving, and education. Minority groups, including Baháís, Christians, and Sunni Muslims, are subject to persecution. Dissenters face imprisonment, torture, or execution for voicing opinions that challenge religious orthodoxy. The Iranian example demonstrates how theocratic regimes prioritize religious conformity over universal human rights, silencing opposition and restricting personal freedoms.[60]

Lebanon: A Divided Governance. Lebanon's political system is built on a delicate balance of power among its major religious groups: Christians, Sunni Muslims, and Shia Muslims. This structure has led to gridlock, as each faction prioritizes its religious interests over national unity. Sectarian conflicts, including a brutal civil war (1975–1990), have left the country deeply fractured and prone to unrest. Reliance on religious quotas in government fosters competition and mistrust, preventing effective governance and sustainable peace.[61]

Historical Lessons on the Fusion of Religion and Governance

Throughout history, the intertwining of religion and politics has often been a precursor to tyranny, persecution, and conflict. For example:

The Spanish Inquisition. A fusion of church and state allowed religious authorities to persecute heretics, Jews, and Muslims under the guise of purifying society.[62]

Colonial America. Before the First Amendment's protections, religious groups often sought to impose their beliefs on entire communities, leading to discrimination against dissenters like Baptists and Quakers.[63]

These historical episodes remind us that religious control of public policy undermines individual freedoms and often paves the way for authoritarianism.

Modern Implications of Religious Control in Public Policy

Erosion of Secular Freedoms. In democracies, attempts to legislate religious morality often lead to the erosion of freedoms. Policies banning abortion or contraception are often justified on religious grounds, disproportionately impacting women. Religious doctrines have been used to justify opposition to marriage equality and anti-discrimination protections for LGBTQ+ individuals. Efforts to introduce creationism or religious teachings in public schools undermine science-based education and alienate students of different beliefs.

Fostering Division and Exclusion. Religious influence in politics fosters an "us versus them" mentality, creating deep rifts in societies. Religious minorities and non-believers often face discrimination or exclusion from public life. Polarization over moral issues, like same-sex marriage or euthanasia, exacerbates political gridlock and erodes trust in institutions.

Domestic Consequences of Religious Influence in the U.S. The dangers are not limited to distant lands. In the United States, policies informed by religious dogma have often infringed on individual freedoms. Anti-abortion laws rooted in religious beliefs have restricted access to healthcare, forcing individuals to adhere to doctrines they may not share. Religious opposition delayed the recognition of same-sex marriage, marginalizing LGBTQ+ individuals. Efforts to teach creationism in public schools reflect attempts to supplant scientific understanding with religious doctrine. Forced display of the 10 Commandments establishes a single dominant religion. These policies illustrate how religious influence in governance has led to the erosion of rights and freedoms, particularly for those who do not share the belief in the dominant faith.

As history demonstrates, governments that uphold secular principles are better equipped to protect human rights, foster inclusivity, and maintain stability in pluralistic societies. The fusion of religion and state, by contrast, often sows division, perpetuates inequality, and endangers democratic ideals.

Historical Leaders' Warnings

"There is no position on which people are so immovable as their religious beliefs. There is no more powerful ally one can claim in a debate than Jesus Christ, or God, or Allah, or whatever one calls this supreme being. But like any powerful weapon, the use of God's name on one's behalf should be used sparingly. The religious factions that are growing throughout our land are not using their religious clout with wisdom. They are trying to force government leaders into following their position 100 percent. If you disagree with these religious groups on a particular moral issue, they complain, they threaten you with a loss of money or votes or both. I'm frankly sick and tired of the political preachers across this country telling me as a citizen that if I want to be a moral person, I must believe in 'A,' 'B,' 'C,' and 'D.' Just who do they think they are? And from where do they presume to claim the right to dictate their moral beliefs to me? And I am even more angry as a legislator who must endure the threats of every religious group who thinks it has some God-granted right to control my vote on every roll call in the Senate. I am warning them today: I will fight them every step of the way if they try to dictate their moral convictions to all Americans in the name of 'conservatism.'"[33,64] —Barry Goldwater

The separation of church and state is a foundational principle in preserving democratic governance, ensuring that no single religious ideology dominates public policy or infringes on individual freedoms. Historically, leaders such as Ulysses S. Grant and Barry Goldwater have championed this divide, warning of the dangers posed by the merging of religious zealotry with political authority.

Grant's Call for Separation. Ulysses S. Grant, a Civil War hero and U.S. president, recognized the importance of keeping religion out of public governance. He famously declared, "Leave the matter of religion to the family altar, the church, and the private school, supported entirely by private contributions. Keep the church and state forever separate." This succinct statement captures the essence of the First Amendment's purpose: to prevent any one religion from gaining undue influence over public life.

Grant understood that religion, while deeply personal and meaningful to many, is best practiced in private spheres. When governments endorse or enforce religious practices, they inevitably infringe on the beliefs of others, undermining the very freedoms democracy seeks to protect.

Goldwater's Conservative Critique. Barry Goldwater, a Republican senator and a stalwart of American conservatism, foresaw the dangers of the Religious Right's growing influence within his party. He warned, "The uncompromising position of these [religious] groups is a divisive element that could tear apart the very spirit of our representative system." Goldwater understood that religious factions, driven by divine certainty, are often unwilling to compromise—a cornerstone of effective governance.

Goldwater's critiques were not theoretical; he witnessed the rise of figures like Jerry Falwell and Pat Robertson, whose Moral Majority movement sought to merge conservative politics with evangelical Christianity. He lamented the takeover of the Republican Party by "a bunch of kooks," warning that this shift would undermine not only the party's principles but also the nation's democratic foundation.

The Rise of Religious Conservatism in U.S. Politics

The Religious Right is a singular threat not just to the conservative political movement but to the Constitution and American values. In 1981, Barry Goldwater warned the United States Senate, "I have spent quite a number of years carrying the flag of the 'Old Conservatism.' And I can say with conviction that the religious issues of these groups have little or nothing to do with conservative politics. The uncompromising position of these [religious] groups is a divisive element that could tear apart the very spirit of our representative system, if they gain sufficient strength. By maintaining the separation of church and state, the United States has avoided the intolerance which has so divided the rest of the world with religious wars."[64,65]

In a 1989 interview, when asked about Pat Robertson and Jerry Falwell, Goldwater said the Republican Party had been taken over by a "bunch of kooks."[66] A few years later he told *The Advocate*, "I don't have any respect for the Religious Right," calling it a "detriment to the country."

Barry Goldwater believed (predicted) in his book *The Conscience of a Conservative* that religious zealots writing laws combining church and government would be the downfall of the United States: "Mark my word, if and when these preachers get control of the [Republican] party, and they're sure trying to do so, it's going to be a terrible damn problem. Frankly, these people frighten me. Politics and governing demand compromise. But these Christians believe they are acting in the name of God, so they can't and won't compromise. I know, I've tried to deal with them."[11]

By blending authoritarian politics with religious fervor, such movements risk creating a government that reflects theocratic tendencies rather than democratic ideals. This echoes the warnings of Goldwater, who feared the rise of factions that claim divine authority to justify their positions, making compromise and pluralism nearly impossible.

Religious Zealotry and Its Political Consequences

Goldwater lived to see his predictions played out by leaders who have used the "conservative" banner to undermine and destroy the fundamental values that he championed.

Ironically, some of these leaders got their start as Goldwater supporters and key conservative strategists such as New Right guru Morton Blackwell and Paul Weyrich.

Paul Weyrich, a fundamentalist Catholic from Wisconsin's right-wing German Catholic community, was one of the most influential conservative strategists in America from the **1970s through the early 2000s.** Inspired by the pro-fascist radio priest Father Charles Coughlin, Weyrich believed that political power in America required two ingredients: *intensity and money.*[67]

While the Republican Party had ample financial support from wealthy donors and corporations, Weyrich saw its lack of grassroots energy as a critical weakness. His solution was to recruit and mobilize conservative evangelical Christians—an untapped base at the time. Working with leaders like Jerry Falwell, Pat Robertson, and James Dobson, Weyrich helped transform cultural and religious issues into political rallying points, including school prayer, creationism, anti-abortion activism, and opposition to LGBT rights.[68,69]

Weyrich co-founded institutions that reshaped American politics, including **The Heritage Foundation (1973)** and **The Moral Majority (1979),** laying the foundation for the religious right's long-term influence in the Republican Party.[70,71] In 1980, he candidly stated:

"I don't want everybody to vote... Our leverage in the elections goes up as the voting populace goes down".[72]

This strategy—mobilize a passionate minority and depress broader turnout—was effective, but also deeply polarizing. Weyrich's legacy continues to shape today's political climate, where ideological purity and cultural warfare often take precedence over compromise and governance.

Political Tactics over Political Discourse

Weyrich's "New Right" has become a dominant political movement that controls the Republican Party. The new Republican Party is held together by authoritarian preachers, mean-spirited TV entertainment news bullies, and zealous podcasters, who constantly whip the Republican base into a fervor through the classic dog whistles of demagoguery: flag-waving patriotism, performative morality, scapegoating of marginalized groups, and manufactured fear. They also rally around selective reverence for the Constitution—particularly the Second and Tenth Amendments—and an idealized version of the Founding Fathers that supports their political narrative.[73]

Sophisticated media smear campaigns have become a defining weapon of the Republican political playbook—deployed not only against Democrats but often within the party itself. This new era of scorched-earth politics took shape in 1988 with Lee Atwater's infamous "Willie Horton"[74] ad, a racially charged piece of demagoguery that helped sink Michael Dukakis. It escalated through the hard-edged partisanship of Newt Gingrich and Tom DeLay and reached new lows with Karl Rove's "swift boating" attacks against critics of the Bush administration. On the media front, figures like Michael Savage, Ann Coulter, Bob Novak, Sean Hannity, Mark Levin, Glenn Beck, and Tucker Carlson amplified the noise with inflammatory rhetoric and baseless accusations branding liberals as traitors. The rise of Bill O'Reilly's primetime dominance on Fox News added even more fuel—his influence on public opinion arguably tipping the scales in favor of George W. Bush during the tightly contested 2000 election.

Weyrich, who launched a culture war not dissimilar to Joseph Goebbels', acknowledged that the New Right was solely focused on power and authoritarian control. "We are radicals who want to change the existing power structure," he wrote in the *Conservative Digest in 1981.*

Pro-business elitist policies became intertwined with authoritarian fundamentalism championed by the Republican Party. The fruit of this labor was the passage of Citizens United.

The Supreme Court's 2010 *Citizens United v. Federal Election Commission* decision fundamentally reshaped the U.S. political landscape by allowing unlimited corporate and individual spending in elections, under the argument that such expenditures are protected as free speech. This ruling has been widely criticized for paving the way for oligarchic influence in democracy, as it amplifies the political power of wealthy individuals, corporations, and special interest groups while diminishing the voice of the average citizen. By equating financial expenditures with speech, Citizens United enabled the formation of Super PACs and dark money networks, which often operate without full transparency and accountability. This influx of unregulated funds has not only deepened economic inequality in the political sphere but also provided a platform for ideological fundamentalism, as well-financed groups can disproportionately shape policy agendas, judicial appointments, and election outcomes. Critics warn that this shift undermines democratic principles, steering governance toward the interests of an elite few at the expense of broader public representation.

Modern Implications: The Threat of Ideological Overreach

Weyrich and Falwell launched the political organization Moral Majority in 1979. In 1980, conservative evangelical Christians helped elect Ronald Reagan to the White House. The Heritage Foundation's 2,000-page manifesto, *Mandate for Leadership*,[75] formed the blueprint for the Reagan administration. The foundation provided research and policy recommendations that influenced Reagan's economic and foreign policy decisions. In particular, the Heritage Foundation advocated for tax cuts, deregulation, and a strong national defense, all of which were key components of Reagan's presidency.

The Heritage Foundation continued to exert influence on politics in the decades following Reagan's presidency. During the George H. W. Bush administration, the foundation played a role in shaping Bush's domestic policy agenda, including advocating for welfare reform and education reform. The foundation also continued to promote conservative principles on issues such as healthcare, immigration, and national security.

In the twenty-first century, the Heritage Foundation has remained a key player in conservative politics. The Heritage Foundation and the Christian Coalition helped engineer the takeover of Congress by Newt Gingrich in 1994.[76] Weyrich's friendship with Karl Rove gave him and the Heritage Foundation unprecedented influence in the George W. Bush administration. The foundation was instrumental in shaping the administration's policies, including advocating for tax cuts, the War on Terror, and conservative appointments to the federal judiciary.[77] The foundation also played a role in shaping the policies of the Trump administration's first term, including advocating for the repeal of the Affordable Care Act, tax reform, and deregulation. The Heritage Foundation's continued influence on Republican administrations is evident in the Trump administration following the latest manifesto, Project 2025.[78]

Project 2025 represents a comprehensive plan to reshape the U.S. government under a conservative framework, aiming for sweeping changes in governance and policy implementation. As a blueprint for a future Republican administration, the project emphasizes consolidating executive power to reduce what it terms bureaucratic inefficiencies. Building on the "Mandate for Leadership" publications, it promotes the unitary executive theory, granting the president increased authority over the executive branch. Central to this plan is the reclassification of tens of thousands of federal civil service jobs to "Schedule F," which would allow the president to replace career officials with politically aligned appointees. Critics warn that this approach could erode the rule of law, diminish the separation of powers, politicize federal agencies, and weaponize the Justice Department, thus compromising their ability to serve the public impartially.

The project's policy goals include dismantling federal agencies such as the Department of Education and Homeland Security, reducing environmental and climate regulations, and promoting socially conservative values. It also advocates for significant tax cuts, curbing labor protections, and restructuring immigration enforcement. These measures have sparked concerns about undermining civil liberties and democratic norms. Supporters argue that such steps are necessary to combat what they view as entrenched resistance within the federal government and to streamline its operations. However, critics highlight the risks of amplifying executive authority and compromising institutional independence, raising alarms about a potential shift toward authoritarianism.

Critics of Project 2025 have also drawn attention to its emphasis on loyalty to the president, which has been interpreted as a direct alignment with former President Donald Trump. By prioritizing personal loyalty over institutional integrity, the plan risks undermining the nonpartisan nature of federal governance. Such restructuring could stifle dissent, suppress diversity of thought, and prioritize political allegiance over merit and expertise. The replacement of career civil servants with politically loyal appointees could jeopardize public trust in government institutions and polarize their operations.

"To announce that there must be no criticism of the President, or that we are to stand by the President, right or wrong, is not only unpatriotic and servile, but is morally treasonable to the American public."[79]—Theodore Roosevelt

Project 2025's active dismantling of regulatory frameworks—particularly in areas such as civil rights protections, labor standards, environmental policies, public health infrastructure, education oversight, LGBTQ+ protections, and immigration enforcement—will severely limit the ability of government institutions to safeguard public accountability. These changes threaten to marginalize Congress and the judiciary, centralizing power within the executive branch and undermining the balance of powers enshrined in the

U.S. Constitution. Critics argue that these shifts not only weaken the democratic process but also pave the way for governance driven by narrow ideological interests rather than the broader public good.

Project 2025 will fundamentally alter the mechanics of governance in the United States. The concentration of power, erosion of transparency, and politicization of public institutions risk destabilizing democratic processes. By prioritizing partisanship and loyalty over expertise and accountability, the initiative could diminish public trust and hinder informed civic engagement, leaving the democratic fabric of the nation increasingly fragile.

History Repeats

Throughout history, authoritarian movements have leveraged fear, propaganda, and centralized power to erode democratic institutions and reshape society to fit their ideological vision. The rise of the "Fourth Reich,"[80] often used metaphorically to describe modern authoritarian movements echoing elements of Nazi Germany, shares striking parallels with the goals and tactics outlined in Project 2025. While the contexts and specifics differ, the patterns of authoritarianism, erosion of civil liberties, and ideological rigidity remain disturbingly familiar.

Attacking Labor Rights and Empowering Elites. One of the hallmarks of the Nazi regime was its systematic dismantling of trade unions and the suppression of workers' rights to consolidate corporate and state power. Workers were deprived of collective bargaining, rendering them vulnerable to exploitation in the name of national productivity and loyalty to the regime. Similarly, Project 2025 advocates for reducing labor protections and promoting pro-business policies under the guise of economic growth. By undermining unions and workers' ability to organize, Project 2025 risks creating a workforce dependent on corporate interests, stripping individuals of economic agency and deepening socioeconomic inequality.

Undermining Science and Rational Thought. The Third Reich aggressively suppressed scientific inquiry that contradicted its racial and ideological dogmas, promoting pseudoscience to justify its policies. A disdain for intellectual discourse and evidence-based decision-making allowed propaganda to flourish unchecked.

Project 2025 mirrors historical patterns by endorsing policies that dismiss scientific consensus on critical issues such as climate change and public health. For instance, the plan advocates for ending "government interference" in energy decisions and promotes the expanded use of oil and natural gas, actions that would accelerate climate change and exacerbate its detrimental health effects. Additionally, Project 2025 proposes significant changes to the federal workforce, including rolling back civil service protections and advocating for the ability to replace current civil servants with individuals who share the administration's ideology. This could lead to the dismissal of experienced scientists and public health officials, undermining the integrity of agencies responsible for safeguarding public health. Such dismissals of objective truths in favor of ideologically driven agendas threaten to weaken public trust in science and pave the way for policies rooted in partisan ideology rather than empirical evidence.[81]

Censorship, Book Banning, and Thought Control. Nazi Germany was infamous for its book burnings and censorship campaigns, which aimed to purge ideas that challenged its ideology. This systematic erasure of dissenting thought stifled intellectual diversity and enforced ideological conformity. In the modern era, Project 2025 aligns with similar trends, such as the push to ban books addressing LGBTQ+ rights, systemic racism, and gender equality from public schools and libraries. These efforts mirror historical attempts to control cultural narratives by silencing opposing voices, creating an echo chamber that marginalizes diverse perspectives and stifles critical thinking.

Demonizing and Oppressing Minorities. The Nazis used propaganda to vilify Jews, Romani people, LGBTQ+ individuals, and other minorities as scapegoats for societal problems, fostering division and justifying oppressive policies.

Project 2025's alignment with socially conservative ideologies risks perpetuating similar patterns by targeting marginalized groups, such as immigrants, women seeking reproductive healthcare, and the LGBTQ+ community.

The Nazi regime's vilification of specific groups extended to policies of mass displacement and state-enforced segregation, targeting communities deemed undesirable or threatening to the regime's vision of a "pure" society. Similarly, Project 2025 embraces rhetoric and policies that portray immigrants as existential threats to national security and cultural identity. Proposals to drastically curtail immigration, accelerate deportation processes, and militarize border enforcement echo historical tactics of scapegoating vulnerable populations for societal challenges. These measures not only erode the humanity of immigrants but also create a climate of fear and division, undermining the pluralistic values foundational to democratic societies. Mass deportation efforts and aggressive immigration restrictions risk destabilizing families, communities, and economies while perpetuating systemic discrimination against those who already face significant barriers to inclusion. Such policies reflect the dangerous legacy of weaponizing national identity to justify exclusion and oppression.

Project 20205 proposed measures to surveil women's reproductive choices, criminalize gender-affirming care, and restrict voting rights disproportionately harm women, reinforce systemic inequality, and foster an exclusionary vision of citizenship.

Eroding Democratic Processes and Centralizing Power. The Nazi regime dismantled democratic institutions, consolidating power within a centralized authority to suppress dissent and enforce ideological conformity. Project 2025's proposals to expand executive power, reclassify civil service positions to allow partisan appointments, and reduce the independence of federal agencies reflect a dangerous drift toward authoritarian governance. These measures threaten to bypass checks and balances, weaken institutional accountability, and undermine the separation of powers enshrined in the U.S. Constitution.

Threats of Violence and Fear as Political Tools. The Nazis relied on violence, intimidation, and threats to enforce compliance and silence opposition. Today, Project 2025's ideological underpinnings include incendiary rhetoric from its proponents, fostering a culture of fear and division. This environment creates a breeding ground for political extremism, as opposition to these ideologies is framed as unpatriotic or immoral. The parallels highlight how fearmongering can be weaponized to justify undemocratic actions while consolidating control over public discourse.

The Danger of Incremental Authoritarianism. Both the Fourth Reich[80] and Project 2025 underscore the danger of incremental changes that cumulatively dismantle democratic norms. While Project 2025 does not openly advocate for authoritarianism, its proposals for restructuring governance, centralizing power, and embedding ideological control in public institutions risk setting the stage for a government that prioritizes loyalty to a singular person over pluralism, accountability, and individual rights. These shifts, like those witnessed in Nazi Germany, exploit democratic systems to subvert them from within, leading to a gradual erosion of freedoms.

A Call for Vigilance. History teaches us that authoritarianism often emerges under the guise of reform, order, or moral renewal. The parallels between the rise of the Fourth Reich and the ideological trajectory of Project 2025 serve as a stark warning. To protect democratic principles, it is essential to recognize and resist these patterns, safeguarding institutions, civil liberties, and the pluralistic values that underpin a free society. Ignoring these lessons risks repeating history's darkest chapters, with devastating consequences for democracy and human rights.

Project 2025, with its potential to align policy with extreme ideologies, could accelerate these trends. The dangers lie not just in overt authoritarianism but in incremental changes that erode civil liberties and institutions over time. Historical parallels underscore the need for vigilance to ensure democratic resilience and prevent a resurgence of totalitarianism in any guise.

Without Government	With Government

Direct Protection

No adequate protection of life	
No adequate protection of family	Police, laws, courts
No adequate protection of property	
No adequate protection of country	Army, Navy, and Air Force

Sanitation and Health

Polluted water	Pure water systems
Filth and waste everywhere	Sewer systems
Tubercular milk	Inspected milk
Disease unchecked	Health services and regulation
Home treatment for diseases	Public hospitals
Impure foods	Pure food and
Dangerous drugs	Drug laws

Education

Private schools for the few	Free education
Unrestricted child labor	Compulsory education
Private libraries	Public libraries

Roads and Conservation

Private mud roads	Highways; rail and air control
Wasted minerals	Mining regulations
Forests burned or destroyed	Reforestation and fire patrols
Pollution of fishing streams	Fish and game regulation
Soil erosion unchecked	Soil conservation

Protection for Business and Labor

Dishonest and unfair practices	Regulation of corporations and unions
Insecure banks	Inspection; deposit insurance
Long hours at low wages	Minimum wages and hours
Dangerous working conditions	Safety and sanitary regulations

Relief

Charity or starvation for unemployed	Public work, security, pensions

Liberty

Oppression by strong and shrewd	Civil rights protected by law

Civilization

Would perish	Needs honesty and efficiency

For Representation of TAXATION

President Eisenhower announced during his first term, "I am conservative when it comes to economic problems but liberal when it comes to human problems."

Fiscally Responsible and Socially Reasonable

One of the most pressing questions for any citizen is whether the services provided by the government are equal in value to the taxes it collects. While the solutions to this question may seem straightforward—focusing on efficient spending and equitable service delivery—partisan politics often complicates efforts to achieve them. A modern republic should prioritize governance that benefits all its citizens equally, emphasizing essential services such as healthcare, infrastructure, and education alongside emergency medical, fire, and police protection. These services should exist as public goods, not commodities driven by profit motives, ensuring accessibility and fairness for every individual.

To achieve this vision, budgeting and spending must be reoriented to reflect the principle of taxation for the people. Government expenditures should be prioritized based on public needs, ensuring that every taxpayer sees tangible benefits from their contributions. A transparent and equitable system would allocate resources efficiently, focusing on public welfare while fostering trust in the institutions responsible for managing public funds. By depoliticizing these efforts and prioritizing outcomes that serve the collective good, citizens can be assured that their taxes are used to build a society where opportunity and security are accessible to all.

One must understand that without taxes there is no support for a government, regardless of whether it is a republic, democracy, or dictatorship. The use of taxes is where our focus should lie, not to abolish all taxes. To simply balance the budget does not provide the fundamental infrastructure and basic services that a government should provide a civilized population. Rational spending of taxes should provide personal welfare via well-trained and well-paid law enforcement, firefighters, schoolteachers, and healthcare providers at the very least. Simply satisfying the basic needs of humanity as studied by Maslow and other scholars of the human condition would ensure each citizen benefits equally from the service of their government.

Human life will never be understood unless its highest aspirations are considered. Growth, self-actualization, the striving toward health, the quest for identity and autonomy, and the yearning for excellence (and other ways of phrasing the striving "upward") must by now be accepted beyond question as a widespread and universal human tendency.[82]

Social Programs Are Not Socialism—They Are Public Service. Social programs are not socialism; they are necessary services that a government is obligated to provide to its people. The U.S. economy is one of free-market capitalism, financed by taxes that keep in check the collective good facilitated by the market. Programs like education, healthcare, and infrastructure are investments in the public doing good, encouraging stability, opportunity, and equity. They do not supplant capitalism; rather, they are added to it as complementary, positively interactive systems, resulting in a holistic mechanism to realign the interests of economic growth with those of society at large, including, of course, globalization.

The Sixteenth Amendment

The Sixteenth Amendment, ratified in 1913, represented a turning point in American history, giving Congress the ability to impose a federal income tax, something that was not only new but aimed primarily at the rich (and not the poor[83,84]). This was a direct response to the rising inequities of the Gilded Age, in which industrial magnates amassed unparalleled wealth while many Americans suffered economic strife. Progressives supported the amendment as a way to level the playing field between wealthy and working-class Americans raising revenue for government programs without relying on regressive taxes—such as tariffs and excise taxes—that disproportionately burden the poor. Rooted in political and judicial battles, the Sixteenth Amendment was. In *Pollock v. Farmers' Loan & Trust Co. (1895)*, the Supreme Court invalidated a federal income tax that had been adopted in 1894, claiming it breached constitutional provisions requiring direct taxes to be apportioned among the states according to their population. It was seen as safeguarding the interests of the rich, meaning income derived from property—especially investments—avoided tax. Many progressives and reformers regarded the ruling as an obstacle to economic fairness.

The Sixteenth Amendment removed this roadblock, providing that if Congress (or the states) did not give apportionment a miss, then incomes—"from whatever source derived"—are subject to tax, thus opening the way for a fairer tax system. The goal of taxing the rich was clear in early income tax laws enacted after the amendment had been ratified. As an example, the Revenue Act of 1913[85] introduced a progressive tax system in which only the richest Americans paid income tax and most Americans did not. This was part of a broader philosophy of Progressive Era reformers who believed that those who could afford higher taxes should contribute more to the public good. For decades, this principle has driven debates around taxation and economic justice, with the Sixteenth Amendment underpinning a program of progressive tax revenue and federal spending that has the specific intent of lowering inequality.

Fair Taxation: Balancing Equity and Simplicity

Taxation has long been a contentious topic, with debates centering on what constitutes fairness in distributing the financial burden of governance. Advocates of a graduated tax system argue that those with higher incomes can and should contribute more to fund public services, as their wealth often depends on the infrastructure, security, and opportunities afforded by a stable society. However, opponents see this approach as punitive, discouraging ambition and penalizing success. These critics often propose a flat tax[86] system as a more equitable alternative.

A flat tax is a taxation system where all taxpayers are charged the same fixed percentage of their income, regardless of how much they earn. Unlike progressive tax systems, which impose higher rates on higher income brackets, a flat tax applies a uniform rate across all levels of income. A flat tax simplifies the tax code, eliminates loopholes, and incentivizes productivity and economic growth by treating all income earners equally. It also reduces administrative costs and makes tax compliance easier for individuals and businesses. A flat tax increases the tax burden on lower-income households, as they pay the same rate without the graduated relief offered in progressive systems. The increased tax burden by lower income earners could be offset by ensuring (with prioritized spending) that their income is not spent on essential needs, such as healthcare, education, and infrastructure.

A flat tax, set at a single rate such as 20 percent, is championed for its simplicity and universal application. It ensures that every individual contributes the same proportion of their income, eliminating the complexity and loopholes that often mar progressive tax systems. By treating all income equally, regardless of its source—be it wages, investments, or inheritances—a flat tax aligns with the principle of equal treatment under the law. Proponents argue this uniformity fosters transparency and trust, removing the perception that certain groups benefit disproportionately from tax breaks or deductions.

This perspective also challenges the notion that the wealthy should bear a disproportionately heavier burden. Critics of graduated systems point to instances where high earners face rates exceeding 50 percent—and historically, even up to 90 percent—which they argue undermines the spirit of free enterprise and personal achievement. When individuals see most of their earnings taxed away, it can create disincentives for entrepreneurship, innovation, and investment. In contrast, a flat tax ensures that success and productivity are rewarded rather than penalized, encouraging economic growth and fostering a culture where all individuals are motivated to achieve their fullest potential.

Furthermore, a simplified flat tax structure reduces administrative overhead, streamlines compliance, and minimizes the opportunities for tax avoidance and evasion. A tax system riddled with exemptions, deductions, and special provisions often favors those who can afford expert accountants or exploit legal ambiguities, perpetuating inequalities that undermine public confidence in the system.

By eliminating these complexities, a flat tax promotes both fairness and efficiency, allowing governments to allocate resources more effectively. According to the Tax Foundation, these costs amount to approximately $546 billion annually, representing 1.9% of the U.S. Gross Domestic Product (GDP).[87] This significant expenditure encompasses the time and resources devoted to tax preparation, including the hiring of tax professionals and the internal processes companies implement to ensure compliance. By simplifying the tax code, businesses could potentially reduce these compliance costs, leading to considerable savings in both time and money.

By avoiding punitive measures on the wealthy, a flat tax respects individual achievements and ensures that prosperity, not redistribution, remains the cornerstone of economic policy. One tax rate, no exceptions, no exemptions, and no exclusions.

The debate over fair taxation reflects broader societal values—whether fairness is defined by equal opportunity, equal contribution, or a redistribution of resources to achieve equity. A flat tax represents an ideological shift toward simplicity, proportionality, and uniformity, challenging the entrenched belief that fairness necessitates graduated burdens. By enacting such a system, proponents argue, society can cultivate an environment where success is celebrated, governance is streamlined, and trust in public institutions is restored.

Taxation For the People: Needs Over Wants

The prioritization of budgeting and spending would ensure each citizen is represented by the taxes paid, **taxation for the people.**

A government budget grounded in Maslow's original theory of motivation, commonly known as Maslow's Hierarchy of Needs,[88] offers a powerful, people-first framework for public spending. By allocating resources in alignment with human needs—from basic survival to personal growth—governments can ensure that taxation reflects the true priorities of a just and forward-looking society.

Maslow's model outlines five tiers of human motivation: Physiological, Safety, Belonging, Esteem, and Self-Actualization. This hierarchy can be translated into a guide for public investment, moving beyond arbitrary political interests toward a systematic approach that enhances well-being, promotes stability, and empowers citizens.

Physiological Needs: The Foundation of Stability. Physiological needs—food, water, shelter, healthcare, and sleep—are essential to human survival and participation in society. In a market economy, many of these are met through employment, but for those unable to access sufficient income, social safety nets such as Social Security, Medicare, Medicaid, unemployment insurance, and food assistance have become essential.

Public health infrastructure is a key pillar: investing in preventative care, mental health, and accessible treatment reduces long-term costs and boosts productivity. Similarly, sustainable housing initiatives reduce homelessness and housing insecurity while spurring local economic growth. Food security programs, agricultural subsidies, and nutrition services for low-income families fight malnutrition and support healthier populations. Finally, water access and sanitation are critical to preventing disease and ensuring equitable development, especially in underserved areas. These investments are not charity; they are the groundwork for a thriving economy and resilient society.

Safety and Security: Protecting the Commons. Beyond survival, people need to feel secure—physically, economically, and socially. Public safety investments in infrastructure maintenance, emergency response, cybersecurity, and defense create the foundation for trust in government and confidence in daily life.

Infrastructure improvements prevent disasters and stimulate commerce, while modern cybersecurity and defense systems protect national sovereignty and digital infrastructure. Climate resilience planning, including early warning systems and disaster preparedness, minimizes long-term damage from natural threats. Meanwhile, economic safety nets—such as unemployment benefits, childcare support, and retirement systems—protect individuals from financial shocks, enabling recovery and long-term stability.

Social Belonging: Building Connected Communities. Humans are social beings, and belonging is essential for mental and social well-being. Investments in public schools, libraries, parks, and community centers foster inclusion and reduce alienation. Programs that promote civic engagement and digital access strengthen democratic participation and social cohesion.

These spaces and programs offer more than services—they provide the connective tissue of society. Governments should prioritize equitable access to these resources, ensuring that every community feels seen, valued, and empowered to contribute.

Esteem: Empowering People to Thrive. Once safety and belonging are secured, individuals seek recognition, dignity, and personal achievement. Governments can support esteem by expanding access to job training, apprenticeships, and education. Workforce development programs and fair labor protections—including equal pay, workplace safety, and enforcement of labor rights—enhance dignity and drive economic mobility.

Public recognition programs, scholarships, and national awards celebrate contributions to society and reinforce a culture of merit and mutual respect. Entrepreneurship support through grants, mentorship, and tax incentives enables innovation and self-determination. These policies send a clear message: everyone's contributions matter.

Self-Actualization: Unlocking National Potential. At the top of Maslow's hierarchy lies the drive for creativity, purpose, and fulfillment. Public spending that supports education, the arts, research, and sustainability creates the conditions for self-actualization. These investments help people explore their passions and push the boundaries of what society can achieve.

Support for cultural programs, scientific research, and innovation hubs cultivates discovery and global leadership. Sustainability initiatives ensure long-term resource availability and demonstrate intergenerational responsibility. A society that funds these aspirations is one that believes in its people and its future.

A Holistic Model for Governance. By aligning taxation and spending with Maslow's hierarchy of needs, governments can foster a resilient, equitable, and future-oriented society. Meeting basic needs is essential, but the work doesn't stop there. True prosperity requires investments that nurture the human spirit, cultivate talent, and build a shared future rooted in dignity and opportunity for all.

This model offers a path beyond reactionary politics—a framework that recognizes governance as a tool for unlocking collective potential.

For CIVIL LIBERTIES

**"The establishment of our new Government
seemed to be the last great experiment for
promoting human happiness."[89]**
—GEORGE WASHINGTON, JANUARY 9, 1790

Civil Rights?

A civil *right* is a right that is asserted and is therefore protected by
some valid law. It may be asserted by common law, or by local or
federal statutes, or by the Constitution; but unless a right is incor-
porated in the law, it is not a civil right and is not enforceable by the
instruments of the civil law.

There may be some rights—"natural," "human," or otherwise—that
should also be civil rights. But if we desire to give such rights the
protection of the law, our recourse is to a state legislature or Supreme
Court ruling or a constitutional amendment.

The history of minority oppression and religious intolerance in
the United States reflects a complex and often painful struggle with
the principles of equality and freedom. Throughout our history,
groups have faced systemic discrimination and exclusion, shaped
by fear, ignorance, and entrenched biases. Women fought for basic

rights such as suffrage and workplace equity, while Black Americans endured centuries of slavery, segregation, and systemic racism that still manifests today. Irish Catholics faced harsh xenophobia in the 19th century, labeled as unfit for democracy, while Japanese Americans were interned during World War II under the guise of national security. Jewish Americans faced anti-Semitism that excluded them from neighborhoods, schools, and workplaces. Today, Hispanics, LGBTQ+ individuals, and other marginalized groups continue to encounter barriers, from voter suppression to workplace discrimination to outright violence.

In 1994, Barry Goldwater led efforts to pass a federal bill banning job discrimination against homosexuals, declared himself an "honorary gay," and observed, "It's time America realized that there was no gay exemption in the right to 'life, liberty, and the pursuit of happiness' in the Declaration of Independence."[90]

Religious intolerance, too, has a deep history in the U.S. During the American Revolution, dissenting faiths often faced hostility from dominant denominations like the Church of England. Over time, Christianity—particularly Protestantism—became culturally dominant, often marginalizing other religious practices. Today, while the First Amendment guarantees religious freedom, many Americans of non-Christian faiths, including Muslims, Jews, Hindus, and others, report experiencing prejudice and discrimination. This underscores a broader societal challenge: the inability to distinguish between tolerating beliefs and endorsing them. To tolerate someone's beliefs means allowing them the space to exist without persecution, even if one disagrees. It does not mean forced acceptance or agreement, nor does disagreement with a belief constitutes persecution.

We must remain vigilant against intolerance and oppression. Teaching the distinctions between inalienable rights and entitlement is critical to addressing these challenges. Inalienable rights, such as freedom of speech and religion, belong to all people and must be protected without exception. Entitlement, on the other hand, refers to specific benefits or privileges granted under law and should be critically examined in the context of fairness and practicality. Similarly, fostering a culture that understands tolerance as coexistence—not forced acceptance or suppression—can pave the way for a more inclusive and harmonious society. Addressing these issues demands commitment to empathy, education, and policy reform, recognizing that while perfection may be unattainable, progress is always possible. This is the cause of America, and anything less would be hypocrisy.

"We have become not a melting pot but a beautiful mosaic. Different people, different beliefs, different yearnings, different hopes, different dreams."[91]—Jimmy Carter

The Constitution is America's enabling document; American citizens are morally and legally obliged to comply with the document. The foundation of our government by the Constitution is anchored in the establishment of rights of its citizens to pursue happiness. The Founding Fathers recognized their limited vision for what the future holds, providing within the Constitution the ability to evolve to meet the needs of the people...to be amended.

Constitutional amendments have extended to include the right to bear arms, women's right to vote, abolishing slavery, abolishing child labor, to name a few. Challenges to our Constitution with the sole purpose to undermine our republic started with its inception and accelerated in the early '50s, continuing to date. To combat this constant attack, we must stand united to counter hate cultures and people that demonize any ethnic group and end systemic racism and misogyny in our society. **Equal rights for all.**

Personal Self-Defense

The Second Amendment stands as a cornerstone of individual liberty, enshrining the right to self-defense as fundamental to the fabric of American democracy. This right is not just a historical relic; it remains a vital protection in a world where safety is not guaranteed, and threats can arise unexpectedly. It is both impractical and unjust to consider disarming law-abiding citizens without simultaneously addressing the root causes of violence that jeopardize their safety. To do so would leave individuals defenseless against potential threats, undermining the very purpose of the Second Amendment.

It is irrational to remove the right for one to defend oneself while not removing the threat. The notion that some neighborhoods are inherently safe while others are plagued by violence is a dangerous illusion. Crime and violence can and do occur in all communities, though they manifest at varying degrees. This reality underscores the necessity of preserving the right to bear arms for self-defense, ensuring that individuals have the means to protect themselves and their loved ones when law enforcement cannot intervene in time. It is a personal right as much as it is a collective safeguard, reflecting the principle that security begins with empowerment at the individual level.

However, the ongoing crisis of gun violence, including mass shootings, requires urgent attention. This is not a problem that should divide Americans into opposing camps of gun proponents and gun opponents. Instead, it is an issue that demands unity, collaboration, and pragmatic solutions. Both sides share a personal stake in reducing violence while preserving constitutional freedoms. Responsible gun ownership legislation, crafted with input from diverse perspectives, can provide a pathway to balance safety and liberty.

A starting point could involve comprehensive research into the causes of gun violence, shedding light on the social, economic, and psychological factors that contribute to this issue. With evidence-based insights, policymakers can design measures that address these root causes without undermining the rights of responsible gun owners. For example, ensuring that firearms are kept out of the hands of those with violent criminal histories or severe mental health issues, through due process and fair systems, could prevent misuse while respecting individual rights.

The conversation about the Second Amendment should not be framed as a zero-sum conflict. Instead, it should reflect a shared commitment to protecting lives and freedoms. By fostering dialogue, building trust, and embracing solutions rooted in common ground, Americans can uphold the right to bear arms while addressing the challenges posed by gun violence. In doing so, the nation affirms its dedication to both liberty and the safety of its people, demonstrating that these principles can coexist harmoniously.

Legislation Equality

The promise of the Fourteenth Amendment[92] and the Civil Rights Act of 1866[93] is foundational to the American ideal of equality under the law. These measures were enacted to ensure that every individual, regardless of race, would enjoy equal rights and protection, including the ability to engage in contracts, own property, and benefit from the full weight of legal safeguards. This principle of legislative equality affirms that all persons possess inherent civil rights, forming a bedrock for justice and fairness in a democratic society. However, these guarantees risk being undermined when laws are inconsistently applied or selectively enforced.

True legislative equality demands that no individual, regardless of their status or position, be exempt from the laws of the land. This includes those within the three branches of government, whose actions must remain subject to the same scrutiny and accountability as those of the citizens they serve. Alarmingly, an emerging divide has placed the ruling class, including oligarchs, elected officials, and influential institutions, above the very laws they create or interpret. This double standard not only erodes trust in governance but also threatens the integrity of democratic systems.

Modern examples of this erosion abound. Laws like the Patriot Act[94], which vastly expanded government surveillance and increased the arrest authority of federal agencies to unprecedented levels, represents a clear intrusion on personal liberties. While aimed at ensuring national security, such legislation often bypasses constitutional safeguards, disproportionately impacting marginalized communities while leaving the architects of these policies largely untouched. Similarly, the absence of enforceable ethics standards for the Supreme Court creates a system where justices wield immense power without meaningful oversight.

The legislative branch exhibits notable disparities in accountability, particularly concerning financial activities. Members of Congress have engaged in stock trading under circumstances that raise concerns about the use of nonpublic information. For instance, in early 2020, several lawmakers faced scrutiny for stock transactions made after receiving confidential briefings on the emerging COVID-19 pandemic. These trades prompted investigations by the Department of Justice and the Securities and Exchange Commission, highlighting potential conflicts of interest and the perception of unequal enforcement of insider trading laws.[95]

In contrast, private citizens have faced severe penalties for similar actions. A prominent example is Martha Stewart, who in 2004 was convicted of conspiracy, obstruction of justice, and making false statements to federal investigators related to her sale of ImClone Systems stock. Although she was not charged with insider trading, her case underscored the stringent application of securities laws to individuals outside the legislative sphere.[96]

In response to public outcry over such disparities, Congress enacted the Stop Trading on Congressional Knowledge (STOCK) Act in 2012.[97] This legislation aimed to prevent insider trading by affirming that members of Congress and their staff are subject to the same insider trading laws as other citizens and required timely disclosure of stock transactions. Despite this, enforcement has been inconsistent, and concerns persist about lawmakers' access to material, nonpublic information and their ability to trade stocks, leading to ongoing debates about the effectiveness of the STOCK Act.[98]

These inconsistencies in accountability contribute to public skepticism regarding the impartiality of the legal system and may erode trust in governmental institutions.

Equally troubling is the precedent set by expanded federal authority through laws like the Patriot Act, which added numerous agencies with arrest powers, including Immigration and Customs Enforcement (ICE) and the Department of Homeland Security (DHS). The sheer scale of this expansion exemplifies government overreach and raises concerns about unchecked authority infringing on civil liberties. These measures, often justified under the guise of national security, blur the line between protecting the public and violating fundamental rights.

Legislative equality must be upheld not only in principle but also in practice. All laws should be applied without regard to race, gender, sexual orientation, or professional status, ensuring that no one is above the law—not members of Congress, not law enforcement, and not the judiciary. Accountability and respect for authority are not mutually exclusive; in fact, genuine accountability strengthens respect by ensuring that those in power act in the public's best interest. Without this commitment to equality and transparency, the democratic foundation upon which the United States is built risks being weakened, leaving its citizens vulnerable to the very abuses the Constitution was designed to prevent.

Education

Education as a civil right aligns with the founding principles of the United States and the values championed by the Founding Fathers. Figures like John Adams and Thomas Jefferson emphasized the importance of public education in sustaining a democratic republic.[99] Adams argued that "a system of general education" was essential for cultivating informed citizens capable of understanding and defending their rights. Jefferson, in his push for publicly funded schools, believed that education would equip individuals with the knowledge necessary to check governmental power and uphold liberty. These early views underscore the foundational belief that education is not merely a private benefit but a public good vital to a functioning democracy.

This principle resonates with the Supreme Court's decision in **Brown v. Board of Education (1954).**[100] The Court recognized the evolving role of education in American life, stating that it is "the very foundation of good citizenship." Chief Justice Earl Warren acknowledged that the Fourteenth Amendment's framers may not have explicitly addressed education, but the Court's mandate was to assess its significance in the modern context. This perspective firmly established education as a civil right, integral to equal opportunity and individual success.

In practice, ensuring affordable and accessible education for all citizens strengthens both individuals and society. Extending education beyond K-12 to include college or vocational training aligns with the Founding Fathers' belief in the civic and economic value of education. For instance, the National Defense Education Act of 1958,[101] created in response to the Cold War's technological race, demonstrated how education serves national security by fostering innovation and skilled expertise.

The challenges of balancing equity and excellence in education remain. Critics of progressive education, such as those influenced by

John Dewey's philosophy,[102] argue that the emphasis on egalitarianism has sometimes limited opportunities for high-achieving students. Yet a balanced approach—combining broad accessibility with pathways for excellence—honors the Founding Fathers' vision while addressing contemporary needs. By affirming education as a civil right and investing in its accessibility and quality, the U.S. ensures its citizens are equipped to uphold democracy, innovate, and thrive.

Limited Government

The government's role in healthcare must respect the fundamental rights of individuals to make personal medical decisions in consultation with their doctors. Decisions about one's body, health, and medical care are deeply personal and should remain free from unwarranted governmental intrusion. Prosecuting or persecuting a woman for adhering to medical advice from her physician, such as seeking an abortion or other reproductive healthcare, represents a clear violation of constitutional protections and personal freedoms. Similarly, while government efforts to ensure public health are important, mandates such as compulsory vaccinations must be carefully limited to scenarios where they demonstrably protect the broader population.

Public health measures, such as requiring certain vaccinations for international travel or to protect vulnerable populations, have historical precedents that demonstrate their value when responsibly applied. For instance, individuals traveling abroad are often required to receive vaccinations to prevent the spread of diseases like yellow fever or typhoid. The case of Typhoid Mary underscores the necessity of balancing individual rights with public health priorities. While isolating her in 1907 infringed on her personal liberties, it was essential to prevent a broader public health crisis. In modern times, herd immunity is a critical concept, as many diseases, including measles, can only be effectively controlled if 95 percent of the population is vaccinated. However, these measures must be rooted in transparency, evidence-based policies, and respect for personal autonomy.

The controversy surrounding reproductive rights exemplifies the tension between personal liberty and governmental overreach. Former Senator Barry Goldwater, a staunch conservative and advocate for individual rights, supported the Supreme Court's landmark 1973 ruling in *Roe v. Wade*. Goldwater believed that a woman's right to make decisions about her pregnancy was a personal matter, free from the interference of religious institutions or political movements. He openly criticized those who sought to impose their beliefs on others, asserting that conservatism is fundamentally about protecting personal freedoms—not dictating moral choices. His stance highlights the critical importance of separating personal medical decisions from political or religious influence.[8]

Goldwater told one interviewer in 1994. "They think I've turned liberal because I believe a woman has a right to an abortion. That's a decision that's up to the pregnant woman, not up to the pope or some do-gooders or the Religious Right."[103]

Vaccination mandates and reproductive healthcare debates share a common thread: They require balanced approaches that prioritize individual rights while protecting collective well-being. The government must tread carefully to avoid overreach, ensuring that public health policies do not infringe upon personal liberties. In the case of vaccinations, the aim should be to educate and encourage participation in public health initiatives rather than resorting to coercion. For reproductive healthcare, the principle is clear: the decision belongs to the individual, not to lawmakers, religious leaders, or activists seeking to impose their beliefs.

Healthcare decisions are not one-size-fits-all, and the government's role should be to provide resources, information, and access, rather than to dictate or restrict options. By respecting the sanctity of the doctor-patient relationship and recognizing the need for balanced public health policies, society can uphold both individual freedoms and collective safety. Protecting these principles ensures that healthcare remains a domain guided by compassion, science, and personal choice—not by political ideology or overreaching authority.

Affordable Healthcare

Access to affordable healthcare is an essential element of a fair and just society and should be recognized not only as a right but as a cornerstone of human dignity. When people cannot access the healthcare they need because of financial barriers, it undermines their ability to fully participate in society and pursue a life of personal fulfillment. The absence of healthcare coverage creates disparities that disproportionately affect vulnerable populations, perpetuating cycles of inequality. Health is intrinsically tied to an individual's ability to contribute to their community, work, and exercise their rights. A person who is unwell or unable to afford medical treatment faces significant challenges in leading a productive life, impacting their family, their community, and the economy at large.

Universal healthcare, where every citizen has guaranteed access to medical care, is the most effective model for ensuring that all people can receive the services they need, regardless of income. Countries such as Canada, the United Kingdom, and many others that have implemented universal healthcare systems offer powerful evidence that providing healthcare as a right not only reduces disparities but leads to better overall health outcomes. By eliminating the financial barriers to care, these systems help ensure that people seek medical attention when needed, often preventing the progression of conditions that could become far more costly to treat later. The focus on preventive care in these systems leads to lower long-term healthcare costs and a healthier, more productive population overall. These nations have shown that healthcare is not merely a service to be bought, but a fundamental component of a society that values the well-being of all its citizens.

The United States has taken steps in this direction with the Affordable Care Act (ACA) of 2010.[104] While not a universal healthcare system, the ACA was a landmark attempt to expand access and reduce disparities in care. By expanding Medicaid, eliminating the practice of denying coverage for preexisting conditions, and providing subsidies to make insurance more affordable, the ACA brought healthcare within reach for millions of Americans who were previously uninsured. While there is still work to be done to achieve universal coverage, the ACA marked significant progress by recognizing healthcare as a right rather than a privilege. It demonstrated that a commitment to expanding access to care, even incrementally, could have a transformative impact on the health and economic stability of individuals, families, and communities.

Recognizing healthcare as a civil right is not just a moral obligation—it is also an economic necessity. When people have access to affordable care, they are healthier and more productive. They are less likely to miss work due to illness or medical bills, and more likely to engage in their communities. Without the financial stress of healthcare expenses, people are better positioned to thrive economically. Furthermore, a population with access to preventive care is less likely to suffer from costly, long-term medical conditions. The financial burden on families and the healthcare system is reduced, and people can focus on living fulfilling lives rather than worrying about how to pay for a doctor's visit.

In a broader sense, universal healthcare strengthens the fabric of a nation by promoting equity and ensuring that every citizen has an equal opportunity to pursue their potential. It is an investment in human capital and societal well-being. If the U.S. were to prioritize affordable healthcare for all, it would not only create a more equitable society but also reinforce the country's founding principles of life, liberty, and the pursuit of happiness for all. By guaranteeing access to healthcare, we ensure that all people have the opportunity to live healthy, productive lives, free from the fear of financial ruin due to medical expenses. Access to healthcare, in this sense, is not merely about the delivery of medical services—it is about providing every person with the tools to succeed, live well, and participate fully in society.

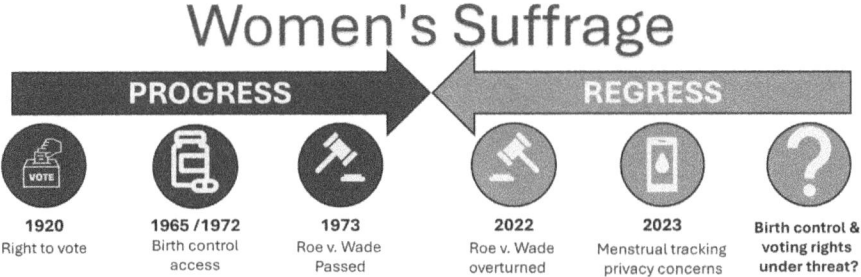

1920	1965 /1972	1973	2022	2023	Birth control &
Right to vote	Birth control access	Roe v. Wade Passed	Roe v. Wade overturned	Menstrual tracking privacy concerns	voting rights under threat?

Women's Suffrage

The history of women's rights in the United States is a story marked by significant struggles, groundbreaking activism, and remarkable progress, though it remains an ongoing journey. The origins of this movement can be traced back to the early nineteenth century, when women began to organize for their rights, often in parallel with the abolitionist movement. The 1848 Seneca Falls Convention,[105] led by trailblazers like Elizabeth Cady Stanton and Lucretia Mott, became a foundational event in the fight for women's suffrage and equal rights. This was the beginning of a long, arduous campaign for gender equality that would span more than seven decades.

Women's suffrage emerged as a pivotal issue for activists throughout the late nineteenth and early twentieth centuries, culminating in the historic ratification of the Nineteenth Amendment in 1920.[106] This amendment granted women the right to vote, marking a monumental victory in the fight for gender equality. Yet, despite this significant achievement, women continued to face systemic discrimination in other spheres of life. The next major milestone came in 1963 with the passage of the Equal Pay Act,[107] which sought to address wage discrimination based on gender, although pay equity would remain an elusive goal for many decades. The Civil Rights Act of 1964 further strengthened the legal framework against gender discrimination in employment, but much work remained to ensure equal treatment for women in all areas of society.

In the 1970s, the fight for women's rights expanded beyond voting and workplace equality to issues of financial independence and educational opportunities. The Equal Credit Opportunity Act of 1974[108] marked a crucial step forward by ensuring that women could obtain credit cards and loans in their own names, without the requirement of a male co-signer. The same year, Congress also outlawed housing discrimination based on sex. Meanwhile, Title IX of the Education Amendments Act of 1972[109] prohibited discrimination in federally funded education programs and activities, greatly expanding opportunities for women in higher education and sports. These legislative victories helped to shape a new era of empowerment for women, where the fight for equality was no longer just about gaining the right to vote, but also about ensuring women could thrive in all aspects of society.

The mid-twentieth century also witnessed the rise of the second wave of feminism, led by prominent figures like Betty Friedan and Gloria Steinem. This movement tackled a broad range of issues, from reproductive rights to workplace equality and societal expectations of women's roles. Supreme Court rulings like *Roe v. Wade in 1973*[110] affirmed a woman's right to make decisions about her own reproductive health, solidifying the legal foundation for women's autonomy over their bodies. Yet even with these legal victories, discrimination and inequality were still deeply entrenched in many areas. In 1981, the Supreme Court ruled that laws that designated husbands as the "head and master" with unilateral control of property owned jointly with their wives were unconstitutional. This was an important legal recognition of women's rights to control their own property and assets.

The late twentieth and early twenty-first centuries saw the expansion of the women's rights movement into new arenas, as women continued to push for broader societal changes. The #MeToo movement,[111] which began in the late 2010s, brought attention to sexual harassment and gender-based violence, galvanizing widespread conversations about power dynamics, consent, and workplace culture. Increasing representation of women in political office and leadership roles reflected the ongoing commitment to achieving full gender equality, with women not only advocating for their rights but also working to ensure that future generations of women would have greater opportunities and protections.

However, despite considerable progress, the fight for women's equality is far from over. Setbacks in recent years have demonstrated the fragility of some of these hard-won rights. In 2022, the Supreme Court overturned both *Roe v. Wade* and *Planned Parenthood v. Casey*, stripping away the constitutional right to an abortion and leaving the regulation of abortion to individual states. This ruling sparked a nationwide debate about women's reproductive rights, with many states passing restrictive laws that criminalize both abortion and the people who seek or provide it. These legal changes have not only severely limited access to abortion services but have also had unintended consequences for other areas of reproductive healthcare, including in vitro fertilization. The reversal of *Roe v. Wade* serves as a stark reminder of how easily rights can be undone and underscores the continued need for vigilance in defending women's rights.

The history of women's suffrage and the broader struggle for gender equality in the U.S. reflects both incredible progress and significant setbacks. The fight for women's rights is not linear, but rather a complex tapestry of legal, cultural, and political struggles. While great strides have been made, the ongoing efforts to ensure full equality for women in all aspects of society remain critical. Women continue to fight for equal pay, comprehensive healthcare, reproductive rights, and an end to gender-based violence and discrimination. The legacy of past generations of activists is carried forward by those who continue to demand that women's rights be upheld and protected for future generations.

Immigration and Minorities

THE NEW COLOSSUS

NOT LIKE THE BRAZEN GIANT OF GREEK FAME,
WITH CONQUERING LIMBS ASTRIDE FROM LAND TO LAND;
HERE AT OUR SEA-WASHED, SUNSET GATES SHALL STAND
A MIGHTY WOMAN WITH A TORCH, WHOSE FLAME
IS THE IMPRISONED LIGHTNING, AND HER NAME
MOTHER OF EXILES. FROM HER BEACON-HAND
GLOWS WORLD-WIDE WELCOME; HER MILD EYES COMMAND
THE AIR-BRIDGED HARBOR THAT TWIN CITIES FRAME.
"KEEP, ANCIENT LANDS, YOUR STORIED POMP!"
        CRIES SHE
WITH SILENT LIPS. "GIVE ME YOUR TIRED, YOUR
        POOR,
YOUR HUDDLED MASSES YEARNING TO BREATHE FREE,
THE WRETCHED REFUSE OF YOUR TEEMING SHORE.
SEND THESE, THE HOMELESS, TEMPEST-TOSSED TO ME,
I LIFT MY LAMP BESIDE THE GOLDEN DOOR!"

EMMA LAZARUS
BORN IN NEW YORK CITY, JULY 22, 1849
DIED NOVEMBER 19, 1887.

The history of the United States' treatment of immigrants and minorities is a complex narrative, marked by periods of exclusion, discrimination, and oppression but also by resilience, resistance, and progress. While the nation was founded on ideals of liberty and equality, these principles often failed to extend to those outside the dominant group—particularly non-white, non-European populations. The legacy of racial, ethnic, and economic hierarchies continues to influence the treatment of minorities and immigrants, shaping both historical and contemporary struggles for justice and inclusion.

From the colonial era, notions of racial superiority influenced policies and practices. Native Americans were displaced through violence, forced assimilation, and legal doctrines like the "Doctrine of Discovery,"[112] which justified land seizure under the guise of divine right. The transatlantic slave trade brought Africans to the colonies, where they were enslaved to sustain agricultural economies. Although slavery was abolished after the Civil War, systemic racism persisted through measures like the Black Codes[113] and Jim Crow laws,[114] which maintained economic and social inequality for African Americans.

Immigrants have faced similar challenges throughout U.S. history. The late nineteenth and early twentieth centuries saw waves of immigrants from Southern and Eastern Europe, who encountered hostility fueled by nativism and fears of cultural and economic disruption. Discriminatory policies, such as the Chinese Exclusion Act of 1882[115] and restrictive quotas in the 1920s, codified these prejudices, limiting immigration from non-European countries and reinforcing the idea of a racially homogenous national identity. Pseudoscientific racial theories during this time bolstered exclusionary attitudes, asserting the supposed superiority of certain racial groups.

Civil rights movements of the mid-twentieth century challenged these inequities. The Civil Rights Act of 1964[116] and the Voting Rights Act of 1965[117] marked significant victories in dismantling segregation and discrimination against African Americans. Similarly, the Immigration and Nationality Act of 1965 abolished racially biased immigration quotas, leading to increased diversity and a shift in the nation's demographic makeup. Despite these advances, racism and exclusion persisted in housing, education, employment, and law enforcement.

In more recent decades, immigration debates have become increasingly polarized. Policies such as the Immigration Reform and Control Act of 1986[118] attempted to address undocumented immigration but often fueled anti-immigrant sentiment. The events of September 11, 2001, intensified xenophobia, particularly against Muslim, Arab, and South Asian communities, who became targets of profiling and hate crimes. Simultaneously, Latin immigrants faced heightened scrutiny, with issues like family separations at the U.S.-Mexico border highlighting the dehumanizing effects of current immigration policies.

Movements like Black Lives Matter have called attention to systemic racism, linking the struggles of Black Americans with broader issues of justice for minorities and immigrants. The Deferred Action for Childhood Arrivals (DACA)[119] program and ongoing debates over comprehensive immigration reform underscore the need for policies that balance security with compassion. The lack of a coherent immigration strategy exacerbates suffering and division, undermining the dignity of migrants and fueling xenophobia.

The United States has made considerable progress in advancing the rights of minorities and immigrants, but substantial challenges remain. Persistent discrimination and a lack of inclusive policies highlight the ongoing struggle for equality. The nation's history serves as both a cautionary tale and an inspiration for continued advocacy, solidarity, and reform to ensure that all individuals are treated with dignity and respect. A humane and pragmatic immigration policy, coupled with efforts to dismantle systemic racism, is essential to fulfilling the promise of liberty and justice for all.

REASONS TO THANK A UNION

1. Weekends
2. All Breaks at Work (Lunch)
3. Paid Vacations
4. FMLA
5. Sick Leave
6. Social Security
7. Minimum Wage
8. Civil Rights Act/ Title VII (Prohibits Discrimination)
9. 8-Hour Work Day
10. Overtime Pay
11. Child Labor Laws
12. Occupational Safety & health Act (OSHA)
13. 40-Hour Work Week
14. Worker's Compensation (Worker's Comp)
15. Unemployment Insurance
16. Pensions
17. Workplace Safety Standards and Regulations
18. Employer Health Care Insurance
19. Collective Bargaining Rights for Employees
20. Wrongful Termination Laws
21. Age Discrimination in Employment Act of 1967
22. Whistleblower Protection Laws
23. Employee Polygraph Protect Act
24. Veteran's Employment and Training Services (VETS)
25. Compensation Increases and Evaluations (Raises)
26. Sexual Harassment Laws
27. Americans With Disabilities Act (ADA)
28. Holiday Pay
29. Employer Dental, Life, and Vision Insurance
30. Privacy Rights
31. Pregnancy and Parental Leave
32. Military Leave
33. The Right to Strike
34. Public Education for Children
35. Equal Pay Acts of 1963 & 2011
36. Laws Ending Sweatshops in the United States

The Middle Class (Labor)

Evaluating a government based on the strength and well-being of its middle class offers critical insights into its effectiveness, stability, and long-term viability. A robust middle class serves as the backbone of a healthy economy, driving consumer spending, innovation, and productivity while fostering social mobility and political stability.

Governments that prioritize policies supporting middle-class growth—such as equitable access to education, affordable healthcare, fair wages, and progressive taxation—demonstrate a commitment to shared prosperity. Conversely, a shrinking or struggling middle class often signals systemic issues like income inequality, inadequate social services, or economic mismanagement. When the middle class thrives, it creates a ripple effect of economic and social benefits, reducing poverty, stabilizing markets, and strengthening democratic institutions by promoting civic engagement and trust in governance. Thus, the state of the middle class is a reliable barometer of a government's success in fostering an equitable and resilient society. The labor movement built the middle class, which was also made possible by strong union representation. We must protect the capitalist environment where people can prosper while keeping it in check to ensure a person does not go broke for the cost of healthcare or an employer refuses to provide a living wage for work performed.

Productive and unproductive labor are concepts that were used in the classical political economy mainly in the eighteenth and nineteenth centuries, which survive today to some extent in modern management discussions, economic sociology, and Marxist or Marxian economic analysis.

Post-Goldwater Republicans, especially since the Reagan era, have gaslighted their people into believing a front-line worker's hourly wage ($15–$45/hour) has more impact on the cost of a product than the CEO's/upper management's ($1,200–$12,000/hour). We must hold employers accountable to pay their workers a minimum living wage. We must protect the workers' right to unionize, to collectively bargain for benefits and compensation that equate to a fair share of the company's profits.

To calculate a living wage, you should consider the costs of basic necessities that allow a worker to support their family while maintaining a modest standard of living. For a person working forty hours per week, the calculation should include the following key budget items:

ESSENTIAL LIVING EXPENSES:

1. **Housing Costs**

   - Average rent for a family of four within twenty-five miles of the worksite.

   - Renters' insurance to ensure stability and protection.

2. **Utilities**

   - Electricity, heating, water, and internet access as it is essential for education and work.

3. **Transportation**

   - Travel expenses, including fuel, basic car payments, and car insurance for commuting to and from work.

4. **Food Costs**

   - A nutritious diet sufficient for a family of four.

5. **Savings**

   - At least 20 percent of total wages allocated toward savings for emergencies, retirement, or future goals.

6. **Healthcare Insurance**

   - Comprehensive coverage for the worker and their family.

Additional Competitive Benefits (If Not Provisioned by Government):

To go beyond basic survival and attract or retain talent while addressing union concerns, employers should also consider:

1. **Education Costs**

    - Contributions toward post-secondary education expenses for the worker to support skill development and career growth.

2. **Childcare Expenses**

    - Affordable childcare options to support working parents.

3. **Stable and Predictable Work Schedule**

    - A schedule that minimizes mandatory overtime to allow for work-life balance.

Including these factors in wage calculations ensures a fair standard of living, improves employee satisfaction, and fosters long-term economic stability.

Unionism, when practiced within its proper and natural boundaries, serves as a positive force in society. Trade unions are vital instruments for achieving economic justice and protecting the dignity of workers. Most importantly, they are expressions of freedom—the inalienable right of individuals to associate and collectively pursue legitimate objectives. Properly functioning trade unions are fundamental to a free society, ensuring employees have a unified voice in bargaining over wages, benefits, and working conditions.

Historically, unions arose out of necessity. As America transitioned from an agrarian economy to an industrial powerhouse in the late nineteenth century, workers faced the immense economic power of large business enterprises. Individual employees, unable to negotiate effectively with their employers, turned to collective representation. Through unity, workers leveled the economic playing field, demanding fair wages and humane conditions. Recognizing the imbalance of power, Congress enacted protections, including the **Clayton Act,**[120] **Norris-LaGuardia Act,**[121] and **National Labor Relations Act (NLRA),**[122] which guaranteed workers' rights to organize and collectively bargain.

However, the effectiveness of unions hinges on maintaining their primary purpose: representing employees in negotiations with their direct employers. When unions stray into unrelated political activities, they risk undermining their legitimacy and focus. For unions to thrive in a free society, they must remain devoted to their foundational role—ensuring fair and equitable employment terms for workers. By doing so, unions continue to balance economic power, foster workplace justice, and strengthen the broader social fabric.

For the Retiree

The issue of retirement benefits for public officials, particularly members of the United States Congress, has been a point of significant discussion and debate, especially in the context of the broader issue of retirement security for ordinary Americans. The congressional pension system, which is made available to members of Congress after they have served for a specified number of years, grants members a pension upon reaching a certain age and service milestones. The pension system for Congress operates under certain conditions that differ from those available to the general public. As of 2019, members of Congress who participate in the pension system are vested after five years of service, meaning they are eligible for benefits after reaching this minimum threshold.

For those who have served for five years, members become eligible to receive their pensions once they reach the age of sixty-two.

Alternatively, if a member has served for twenty years, they can begin receiving pension benefits at the age of fifty. For those with twenty-five years of service, the pension becomes available at any age, providing significant flexibility. However, the pension amount can be reduced based on the specific age or years of service under different conditions, depending on how the individual member has structured their retirement benefits. Additionally, if a member of Congress decides to leave office before reaching retirement age, they can leave their contributions behind and still receive a deferred pension at a later date.[123]

This congressional pension system stands in contrast to the retirement plans available to most American workers, who primarily rely on Social Security and private retirement savings. Social Security is designed to serve as a safety net for retirees, but many Americans face challenges with its adequacy given the rising cost of living and increasing healthcare expenses. The eligibility age for "full" Social Security benefits is currently set at sixty-seven for those born after 1960, with an option for early retirement at age sixty-two, though this results in a reduction in monthly benefits.

Proponents of reforming the U.S. retirement system often argue that every American should be afforded the same level of retirement security and benefits that are available to members of Congress. One way to ensure more equitable retirement opportunities for all citizens is to lower the eligibility age for Social Security to sixty. This adjustment would better reflect the realities of modern life, in which many people are unable to work past a certain age due to health issues or the physical demands of their careers. Lowering the eligibility age would ensure that more people can access their benefits earlier and with fewer financial struggles during retirement.

Another potential reform is to reinstate employer-sponsored retirement plans, such as pension plans, to a level that mirrors the benefits provided to Congress members. Historically, employer-sponsored pensions were more common, but many employers have shifted toward offering 401(k) plans instead, which often place more responsibility on employees to save for their own retirement. For many workers, the shift to 401(k)-style plans has not been as beneficial as pension plans, which provide more certainty and stability. Reintroducing pension plans or similar employer-backed retirement options could provide a stronger safety net for American workers, helping them to retire with more financial security and reducing their dependence on government programs like Social Security.

The issue of fairness in retirement benefits, especially when comparing the benefits enjoyed by Congress members to those available to the general population, is one that sparks significant discussion. Many Americans find it difficult to reconcile the differences in pension systems between elected officials and themselves. While the pension plans for members of Congress are often seen as a form of compensation for their public service, critics argue that these generous benefits should not be exclusive to politicians but should instead be available to all citizens who contribute to society throughout their careers.

If we are to ensure that every American has a secure and dignified retirement, we must consider expanding and strengthening Social Security and employer-sponsored retirement options. Reducing the eligibility age for Social Security to sixty would be a first step in addressing the growing disparities in retirement security. Additionally, bringing back robust employer pension plans would offer workers the stability and certainty they need as they approach retirement age. These changes would provide a more equitable system that offers every American the opportunity to enjoy a secure and comfortable retirement, regardless of their career path or income level.

The question of how to ensure better retirement options for all Americans cannot be viewed in isolation from the broader challenges facing the nation's economic future. Rising income inequality, changes in the nature of work, and the increasing burden of healthcare costs are all factors that contribute to financial insecurity for many older Americans. In response, reforming the retirement system to provide fairer access to retirement benefits—mirroring the advantages enjoyed by elected officials—could help restore faith in the nation's commitment to the well-being of its citizens, especially as they age. By ensuring that all citizens can retire with dignity, we uphold the principles of equality and justice that the United States was founded upon.

For NATIONAL SECURITY

"Do I not destroy my enemies when I make them my friends?"
—ABRAHAM LINCOLN

Threat Assessment: Domestic and Abroad

The Pentagon's 2024 Annual Threat Assessment (ATA)[124] [Unclassified] highlights a wide range of challenges to U.S. national security, reflecting a complex and dynamic global environment. The ATA identifies key threats including the evolving capabilities of state adversaries like China, Russia, North Korea, and Iran. China remains a top concern, with its ambitions for global economic dominance, advancements in military modernization, and assertive behavior in the Indo-Pacific. Russia's "acquisition" of Crimea, ongoing aggression in Ukraine, and nuclear saber-rattling continue to destabilize Europe and challenge U.S. and NATO strategies. North Korea's nuclear and missile advancements, coupled with its strengthening ties to Russia, underscore the persistence of this threat. Meanwhile, Iran's regional influence, including support for proxy groups, remains a critical issue, though the ATA notes a lack of direct involvement in recent escalations, such as the Hamas attacks in Israel.

Beyond state actors, the report underscores risks from cyber operations targeting U.S. infrastructure, transnational organized crime, and climate-related challenges that exacerbate global instability. Terrorism remains a concern, with non-state actors continuing to adapt their tactics. The assessment also cautions that U.S. actions, such as military buildup or sanctions, may sometimes be interpreted by adversaries as escalatory, potentially triggering counteractions. These insights aim to inform policymakers on the complexities of mitigating threats while balancing strategic and diplomatic objectives.

The ATA emphasizes the need for vigilance, innovation, and international collaboration to address these multifaceted security challenges effectively. It serves as a foundational tool for shaping U.S. defense and foreign policy in an increasingly interconnected and contested world.[9, 10]

Observations from the ATA 2024

THREAT ASSESSMENT: REGIONAL AND GLOBAL ACTIVITIES

The geopolitical landscape is currently shaped by a complex mix of regional and global activities that reflect shifting power dynamics, with a focus on strategic challenges posed by nations like China, Russia, Iran, and North Korea. Each of these countries continues to pursue its own vision of power and influence, often at odds with U.S. interests, regional stability, and global order.

China, under the leadership of President Xi Jinping, envisions a future in which the country holds the position of preeminent power in East Asia and is a leading player on the world stage. The Chinese Communist Party (CCP) aims to undermine U.S. influence globally, while simultaneously working to drive wedges between the United States and its international partners. One of the most significant challenges in the U.S.-China relationship is China's aggressive stance toward Taiwan. The People's Republic of China (PRC) continues to press for unification with Taiwan, a move that would create critical friction points with the United States, which maintains its commitment to Taiwan's security. Despite facing internal economic setbacks, China's leadership remains resolute in its approach to economic policy, with an emphasis on reducing dependence on foreign technologies and fostering indigenous innovation. These policies serve as a foundation for military modernization, intending to increase China's global influence and solidify its position as a regional hegemon.

Russia, meanwhile, has taken a confrontational approach to its international relations, particularly with its aggressive actions toward Ukraine. The annexation of Crimea in 2014 marked a critical turning point, signaling Russia's willingness to challenge international norms and redraw borders by force. Since then, Russia has maintained an active role in eastern Ukraine, supporting separatist movements and engaging in military interventions. In February 2022, Russia escalated its aggression by launching a full-scale invasion of Ukraine, aiming to undermine Ukrainian sovereignty and challenge the post-Cold War security order in Europe. Beyond Ukraine, Russia has extended its influence through hybrid warfare tactics, including cyberattacks, disinformation campaigns, and military involvement in countries like Syria. Its strengthening ties with nations such as China, Iran, and North Korea have further complicated the global security landscape. These alliances serve to bolster Russia's defense production and economy, challenging U.S. and NATO interests and creating a more complex web of confrontational policies and alliances. The use of energy as a coercive tool, alongside cyber operations, and espionage, is expected to remain central to Russia's strategy, as it continues to undermine Western unity and exert influence in post-Soviet states.

Iran, while less powerful than China or Russia on the global stage, plays a significant role in shaping regional dynamics, particularly in the Middle East. Iran's goal is to entrench itself as a dominant regional power while minimizing threats to the regime. Over the years, Iran has leveraged its military successes and expanded its nuclear program to assert its ambitions, drawing closer to Russia for diplomatic and defense cooperation. Tehran's support for militant groups, including Hezbollah and Hamas, and its involvement in regional conflicts such as those in Syria and Iraq, has consistently positioned Iran as a threat to U.S. allies, particularly Israel. Iran has also used the Gaza conflict to further its narrative of opposition to Israel, attempting to galvanize support among other Middle Eastern nations and present itself as the defender of the Palestinian cause. Iran's regional activities, including arming proxy groups and supporting movements that challenge U.S. influence, ensure that it will remain a persistent threat to regional stability and U.S. interests in the Middle East.

North Korea, led by Kim Jong Un, continues to pose a significant threat through its development of nuclear and conventional military capabilities. Despite facing intense international sanctions and self-imposed isolation due to the COVID-19 pandemic, North Korea has been able to reemerge as a player in the geopolitical sphere. The country has strengthened its military ties with both China and Russia, aiming to secure diplomatic support and increase its defense cooperation. Kim Jong Un's regime seeks international acceptance as a nuclear power, which poses a direct threat to the United States and its allies in the region. The ongoing development of nuclear weapons and missile technology, combined with a history of periodic provocations, ensures that North Korea remains a destabilizing force in East Asia. Its growing ties with Russia and China complicate efforts by the U.S. and its allies to isolate the regime and prevent further nuclear proliferation.

The Gaza conflict, which escalated dramatically in October 2023 with a major Hamas attack on Israel, has intensified regional tensions.

Israel's military response, aimed at neutralizing Hamas and other militant groups, has resulted in significant loss of life and widespread destruction in Gaza. The violence has been amplified by a robust social media campaign, further fueling global divisions and intensifying public scrutiny. Iran-backed militant groups in the region have used the situation as an opportunity to attack U.S. interests, leveraging the conflict to destabilize neighboring countries like Lebanon, Iraq, and those in the Gulf. Israel, already facing international condemnation over its military actions, is under increasing pressure to address the humanitarian crisis in Gaza, while Iranian proxies continue to push their agenda of anti-U.S. and anti-Israel rhetoric. The conflict is likely to have long-term repercussions on regional stability, with Iran seeking to undermine U.S. influence and prevent Middle Eastern states from normalizing relations with Israel.

Together, these regional and global activities represent a multi-faceted challenge to U.S. influence and security. The shifting power dynamics, driven by the actions of China, Russia, Iran, North Korea, and the ongoing Gaza conflict, present a complex web of threats that the United States and its allies must navigate. These challenges are compounded by the increasing use of hybrid warfare, cyber operations, and disinformation campaigns, which complicate traditional diplomatic responses. As global tensions rise, the need for strategic coordination and careful diplomacy has never been more crucial in maintaining international stability and safeguarding democratic values.

CYBER THREATS FROM IRAN, CHINA, AND RUSSIA

Iran has consistently employed cyber operations as part of its broader strategy to advance its geopolitical and security objectives. Tehran's cyber campaigns are multifaceted, targeting various domains including espionage, influence operations, and direct attacks on critical infrastructure, both within the Middle East and beyond. While Iran's cyber capabilities are not as advanced as those of Russia or China, they have grown significantly in recent years, allowing Tehran to conduct increasingly sophisticated operations. One of the main focuses of these cyber activities is destabilizing adversaries, particularly the U.S. and its allies in the Middle East. Iranian cyber groups have been linked to a series of high-profile cyberattacks aimed at financial institutions, energy sectors, and government agencies, often with the goal of disrupting economies and sowing discord. Ransomware attacks have become a notable tool in Iran's arsenal, allowing for both financial extortion and targeted disruptions. Additionally, Iranian hackers have been implicated in spreading disinformation campaigns, particularly aimed at amplifying anti-Western sentiment and fostering unrest within expatriate communities. These efforts often align with Tehran's broader strategic aims of weakening the influence of Western powers in the region and reinforcing its own narrative against perceived foreign interference. By leveraging cyber tools, Iran can reach across borders to influence public opinion, support proxy activities, and advance its political and security agenda in ways that would be harder to achieve through traditional diplomatic or military means.

China, on the other hand, has developed one of the most expansive and sophisticated cyber strategies in the world. The Chinese government uses cyber operations to achieve a range of economic, military, and political objectives, with a clear focus on bolstering the country's global power. Chinese cyber operations are known for targeting intellectual property, with the theft of trade secrets being a primary goal. By acquiring valuable technologies and information, China aims to accelerate its domestic industries and advance its military capabilities. This includes stealing data from U.S. government agencies and private corporations, as exemplified by the massive breach of the Office of Personnel Management, which exposed sensitive information about millions of American citizens. Such breaches are indicative of China's persistent efforts to gain intelligence on foreign governments, military strategies, and key economic sectors. Beyond espionage, China's cyber capabilities also include a comprehensive domestic surveillance system, enabling the government to monitor and control its own population with an unprecedented level of precision. Internationally, China uses its cyber tools to shape narratives, censor content, and conduct influence operations, particularly in regions like Taiwan, Hong Kong, and the South China Sea. Cyber campaigns have been used to promote Beijing's version of events and suppress dissenting voices, influencing foreign audiences and governments while simultaneously stoking tensions in contested regions. By combining state-sponsored cyber operations with its broader political objectives, China seeks to enhance its position both domestically and globally, while also complicating efforts by adversaries to counter its growing influence.

Russia's approach to cyber warfare is notably disruptive and destabilizing, with a clear emphasis on undermining the security and stability of Western democracies. Russian cyber operations often involve direct interference with political processes, including the notorious interference in the 2016 U.S. presidential election. By deploying sophisticated disinformation campaigns and cyberattacks, Russia aims to polarize societies, erode public trust in institutions, and create confusion among political opponents. This is part of a broader strategy to weaken the political cohesion of rival nations and diminish their ability to effectively counter Russian actions on the global stage. Russian cyber tactics go beyond information warfare and have increasingly involved targeting critical infrastructure, such as energy grids and transportation systems. These attacks demonstrate Russia's willingness to integrate cyber capabilities with conventional military strategies, using the digital realm to destabilize the systems that underpin modern society. In the context of the ongoing war in

Ukraine, Russian hackers have targeted both civilian and military systems, disrupting essential services and attempting to disrupt Ukraine's ability to function as a state. These operations have become an integral part of Russia's broader geopolitical aggression, highlighting the importance of cyber warfare in modern conflicts. Russia continues to test the boundaries of international norms and agreements; cyber operations are likely to remain at the core of its efforts to create civil disturbance in the West and expand its influence in the world.

Together, these countries highlight the growing significance of cyberspace in international conflicts. Although each nation has its own unique approach and strategic vision, their use of cyber capabilities reflects a broader trend of utilizing digital tools to achieve objectives that previously could only be met through traditional military or diplomatic means. Cyberattacks, disinformation campaigns, and surveillance have become central components of the geopolitical strategies employed by countries such as Iran, China, and Russia. These strategies enable them to advance their goals while complicating efforts by adversaries to secure influence.

The cyber domain is inherently dynamic, and as it continues to evolve, the threats posed by state-sponsored cyber operations are likely to increase. Therefore, defense leaders must devise comprehensive strategies to counter and mitigate the effects of such covert actions. Given their significance, international cooperation, along with established norms and regulations regarding the use of cyber capabilities in pursuit of national interests, is becoming increasingly important.

DISRUPTIVE TECHNOLOGIES AND MALIGNED INFORMATION

Emerging technologies, especially artificial intelligence (AI) and quantum computing, are transforming the global security landscape and are being weaponized by state actors including China, Russia, and Iran. Instead, this threat comes from an attacker with far more powerful tools and arms than ever before—AI, capable of processing and generating content on a scale and at a pace hitherto unimaginable. When it comes to disinformation, AI can be used to generate highly convincing fake content—including deepfake videos, synthetic images, and fabricated audio—that closely mimics real people and events. These technologies enable malicious actors to produce content so realistic that it becomes increasingly difficult for the public to distinguish fact from fiction. This fictitious information shapes public opinion, creates confusion, propagates falsehoods, and influences elections and political agendas. To make matters worse, AI can produce automated news articles, fake social media accounts, and other types of propaganda that make it possible to spread disinformation on an industrial scale, thus making it more difficult for the public to tell what is real and what is fake, inflaming conspiracy theories. This trend is not limited to rogue groups or lone-wolf actors; similarly, state actors are adopting AI solutions as tools through which nations like Russia, China, and Iran can strategically pursue their own geopolitical agendas and compromise the integrity of democratic institutions around the world.

Another emerging technology that raises security concerns is quantum computing. This could be alarming, as quantum computing can break the encryption algorithms currently used—algorithms that underpin the security of the entire planet, global cybersecurity, and protection of sensitive information. While the technology itself is in its early stages, with no commercially viable systems yet in existence, its implications are enormous, potentially putting existing encryption protocols out of business and exposing everything from government communications to private financial transactions. Quantum computing could, in the hands of adversaries, compromise national security, corporate intellectual property, and individual privacy on a global scale by allowing them to decrypt massive amounts of sensitive information. Competitive quantum computing development has already commenced, with technologically well-resourced nations working to gain a comparative advantage over their adversaries. This shift represents another front where the disruptive technologies of tomorrow cross swords with war machines of the past when the winning of nations came down to who had the better technology.

Manipulation of information has emerged as a central part of the statecraft of many countries. In recent decades, the manipulation of information has evolved from traditional propaganda into a powerful branding tool on social media. State-sponsored actors and domestic influencers now use these platforms to spread tailored messages—targeting even the smallest social groups and psychological vulnerabilities with precision and repetition. Manipulators have also become highly skilled at exploiting Facebook, Twitter, YouTube, and other social media to spread false narratives, shape public opinion, and sow discord in democratic societies. The 2016 U.S. presidential election is a prime example of how disinformation may interfere with democratic processes, as Russian operatives conducted an extensive online effort to interfere with the electoral process. In addition to undermining elections, Russian trolls and bot networks have been used to complicate public health campaigns—especially regarding vaccine misinformation—and to continue polarizing political discourse. These tactics destabilize the internal political landscape while they erode faith in democratic institutions and processes leading to fragmentation in the longer run.

China has similarly embraced information warfare, albeit with a slightly different focus. The Chinese government has long utilized its extensive digital surveillance capabilities to control domestic narratives, but it has also extended these efforts globally, particularly around contentious issues such as Taiwan, Xinjiang, and the Belt and Road Initiative. By controlling the narrative surrounding these topics,

China seeks to influence public opinion and diplomatic relations on the global stage, often through censorship and the promotion of state-sponsored narratives. China's information operations have been strategically deployed to shape perceptions in both developed and developing countries, using social media platforms, online news outlets, and academic publications to advance the country's political objectives. These efforts reflect China's broader goal of establishing itself as a global leader in the twenty-first century while challenging Western democratic values and norms.

Although Iran lacks the technological sophistication of Russia and China, it also engages in information warfare as a means of furthering its ideological agendas, while resisting U.S. dominance of the Middle East. The Iranian regime has a history of abusing social media platforms to spread anti-U.S., anti-Israel rhetoric, especially after they have erupted regionally, most significantly at the sites of the Israeli-Palestinian dispute. Iranian disinformation efforts tend to seek to unify its own population and its regional allies and destabilize its foes. This way, Iran hopes to establish internal and international pressure on Western governments, contributing to its geopolitical game throughout the region, while turning back sectarian divisions and forming conspiracy theories. Further, Iran's disinformation campaigns, although less sophisticated than those launched by Russia or China, are still impactful on regional stability and global perception, especially within the context of the Middle East's volatile political environment.

This trifecta of cyber aggression, tech innovation, and info war could potentially upend global stability and erode democratic governance. The ability of state actors to exploit emerging technologies to further their strategic goals highlights the vulnerability of modern societies in the new digital age. Such measures go well beyond direct military clashes and attack the heart of democratic structures, from election procedures to public faith in the media and government. Emerging technologies such as AI and quantum computing, combined with the proliferation of disinformation, make for an incredibly complex and volatile environment where the traditional geopolitical toolkit is augmented with digital tools. For democracies, these threats make for an urgent imperative to build strong cyber-secure regimes, regulatory frameworks, and international collaboration to protect against threats.

With these technologies serving as mere harbingers of more sophisticated tools to come, the potential for misuse will only increase, and it will become increasingly essential for leaders around the world to do what they can to safeguard their societies. We will need to address the challenges of disruptive technologies and maligned information and advance this work to build the technologies to mitigate the risks of such technologies to society and reform policies that ensure exuberant information spread and innovation while being safe. In an era where warfare and influence are waged through code rather than conventional arms, defending democracy requires a new kind of vigilance. Adversaries are targeting the digital infrastructure that underpins our democratic institutions—the virtual equivalent of bricks and mortar. As the lines between the physical and digital worlds continue to blur, protecting our systems will demand unprecedented levels of cooperation, adaptability, and sustained attention.

CLIMATE CHANGE AND EXTREME WEATHER

Climate change and extreme weather are increasingly recognized as significant threats to U.S. national security, as their effects reach beyond environmental damage to deeply impact economic stability, military readiness, and geopolitical dynamics. Rising global temperatures and sea-level increases are intensifying the occurrence and severity of extreme weather events, including hurricanes, floods, wildfires, droughts, and heat waves. These disruptions directly affect critical infrastructure, such as transportation networks, power grids, and water supplies, while also threatening military facilities, particularly those located in coastal regions. Flooding, for instance, poses a severe risk to coastal military installations, damaging facilities and equipment and rendering them unfit for immediate use in national defense operations. Extreme weather events, which are becoming more frequent and intense, further strain infrastructure, making it more difficult to respond to both environmental disasters and security threats, and also posing a challenge to long-term military readiness.

The growing unpredictability of weather patterns, along with the increasing severity of natural disasters, has a direct impact on the ability to maintain stable and productive agricultural systems, which are vital for both domestic consumption and global food supply. In many regions, droughts and heat waves are reducing the availability of water resources and agricultural yields, creating competition for these increasingly scarce resources. This scarcity, compounded by the effects of climate change, can heighten tensions within and between nations, fueling economic instability and triggering conflicts over access to vital resources such as water, food, and energy. Competition for these resources can destabilize entire regions, particularly in parts of the world that are already vulnerable, setting the stage for conflicts that may demand military intervention or humanitarian response.

The destabilizing effects of climate change also exacerbate existing vulnerabilities in societies, particularly in less developed regions. For instance, rising temperatures and erratic weather patterns can reduce crop yields and disrupt supply chains, undermining economic livelihoods. Communities dependent on agriculture and fishing for their survival are particularly susceptible to such disruptions, which can lead to displacement and an increased risk of violence. The resulting displacement often creates refugee crises, which in turn can destabilize neighboring countries and place additional strain on international institutions and humanitarian organizations. As populations are forced to migrate due to climate-related pressures, the social and political dynamics of receiving countries are strained, leading to increased tensions, potential radicalization, and the emergence of extremist groups that may exploit instability for their own gain. The ripple effect of these challenges can extend far beyond the immediate regions impacted by climate change, spreading to other parts of the world and exacerbating global security risks.

As climate change accelerates, it also magnifies the complex intersection of environmental, economic, and geopolitical risks. For instance, the melting of Arctic ice is creating new opportunities for resource extraction and new trade routes, but it is also intensifying geopolitical competition. Nations such as Russia, the U.S., and China are increasingly eyeing the Arctic as a strategically significant region due to its untapped resources, including oil, gas, and rare earth minerals, as well as its potential to open new shipping lanes that could reshape global trade routes. The thawing ice is leading to increased military presence in the region, as countries assert their claims over new territory and seek to gain a strategic advantage. This intensifying competition over the Arctic reflects how environmental change is intertwining with geopolitical and economic considerations, creating new sources of tension and conflict that could have far-reaching implications for global security.

In addition to these external risks, the United States itself is feeling the effects of climate change on its national defense priorities. The U.S. Department of Defense (DoD) has recognized climate change as a critical national security concern,[125] one that directly affects military operations, personnel, and infrastructure. The DoD has begun incorporating climate adaptation strategies into its military planning to ensure that its forces remain prepared for the challenges posed by a changing climate. For example, the military is adapting its infrastructure and logistics to cope with increasingly frequent and severe natural disasters, such as hurricanes and floods, which can disrupt operations and jeopardize national defense capabilities. Furthermore, the U.S. military is becoming more involved in disaster relief and humanitarian aid missions, as climate-induced disasters force greater demands on U.S. forces to provide assistance both domestically and abroad.

These increased demands on military resources underscore the growing intersection between climate change and national security, making it clear that climate change is not just an environmental issue but a security issue with the potential to strain military capabilities and international relations. The broader implications of climate change for global stability are profound, as the interplay of resource scarcity, displacement, and instability can fuel geopolitical rivalries, cause mass migration, and contribute to the rise of conflicts in regions that are already fragile. The U.S., with its global interests and commitments, will need to address these emerging risks through a multifaceted approach, focusing not only on military readiness but also on diplomatic, humanitarian, and economic strategies that aim to mitigate the effects of climate change while maintaining national and global security.

The impacts of climate change on U.S. national security are far-reaching, affecting everything from military infrastructure and strategic resources to global geopolitical stability. As temperatures rise, sea levels increase, and extreme weather events grow more frequent, the U.S. and its allies face a complex array of challenges that require integrated strategies to ensure long-term security. The effects of climate change, from destabilized regions to increased resource competition, highlight the urgent need for both national and international cooperation to address the multifaceted risks posed by this global crisis. Given that climate change is a threat multiplier, compounding existing vulnerabilities and creating new ones, it is critical that the U.S. continues to prioritize climate adaptation in its defense planning and engage with global partners to strengthen resilience against the security risks posed by a rapidly changing climate.[126,127]

PLUTOCRATIC OLIGARCHY: NEO-FASCISM

The rise of a plutocratic oligarchy in the United States represents a significant threat to the democratic foundations upon which the country was built. This shift, where power and wealth have become increasingly concentrated in the hands of a small elite, erodes the principle of equal representation, a core tenet of democracy. Over recent decades, the divide between the rich and the rest of society has grown more pronounced, with the wealthiest Americans accumulating a disproportionate share of the nation's economic resources. This accumulation of wealth has allowed the elite to exert profound influence over the country's political system, often at the expense of the public good. The concentration of power in the hands of a few means that policy decisions increasingly reflect the interests of this wealthy minority, leaving broader societal needs, such as the fight against income inequality, climate change, and the provision of public health, neglected.

It is especially visible in the shaping of policy priorities. The political and economic system has been increasingly molded to serve the interests of large corporations and the ultra-wealthy, often at the expense of policies that would benefit the general public over time. Tax cuts for corporations, deregulation of industries, and policies that favor capital accumulation among the richest Americans are prime examples of how the interests of the wealthiest have taken precedence over those of the majority. While these policies have fostered economic growth, they have also contributed to rising inequality and a weakening of the public sector, which is essential for ensuring that the needs of all citizens are met.

One of the most salient contributing components to the growth of plutocracy in the U.S. has been the role of money in politics, particularly after the Supreme Court's 2010 *Citizens United* decision. This landmark ruling unleashed a torrent of unchecked corporate spending on elections on the grounds that corporate political spending is a form of free speech protected by the First Amendment. They argue that the ruling has subverted democracy, allowing the wealthy and business interests to drown out the voices of everyday Americans. The approval has led to a situation in which the interests of the wealthy elite can overtake political discourse, dictating outcomes and public policy in a manner that serves their coffers as opposed to the public interest. Such erosion has resulted in a condition in which elected officials are, more often than not, responsive to those who make large donations rather than to their constituents.

In addition, the revolving door between public office and the private sector continues to accelerate the slide toward plutocracy. Politicians and government officials frequently rotate between regulatory roles and lucrative positions in the very industries they once oversaw. A notable example is when former ExxonMobil CEO **Rex Tillerson** was appointed as Secretary of State, or when former oil and coal lobbyist Andrew Wheeler was tapped to lead the **Environmental Protection Agency (EPA)**—an agency tasked with regulating the very industries he previously represented. These appointments raise serious concerns about conflicts of interest, as officials may shape policy in ways that benefit future employers or reward past associations. Public service, in such cases, becomes less about serving the people and more about securing future wealth. This undermines trust in public institutions and erodes the integrity of the political system itself.

Efforts to address the growing influence of plutocratic oligarchy and the increasing role of money in politics have gained traction among reformers. Proposals for campaign finance reform, such as limiting private donations to political campaigns, are central to efforts to restore balance to the political system. Advocates argue that reducing the influence of money in politics is essential to ensuring that elected officials represent the interests of the broader electorate, rather than just the wealthy few. Transparency measures, such as requiring greater disclosure of donors and lobbying activities, would allow voters to better understand the sources of political influence and hold elected officials accountable for their actions. Additionally, efforts to close the revolving door between public office and the private sector, through stronger conflict-of-interest laws and regulations, could reduce the risk of corruption and ensure that public servants act in the best interests of their constituents.

Beyond policy reforms, there is a growing call to address the root cause of plutocratic control: the widening wealth gap. The increasing concentration of wealth among the top 1 percent has led to a situation where the economic and political power of the few threatens to undermine the fundamental principles of democracy. Advocates for economic equality argue that reducing this wealth gap is essential to fostering a true democracy where all citizens have an equal opportunity to participate in the political process and have their voices heard. This includes policies aimed at addressing income inequality, such as raising the minimum wage, expanding access to education, and reforming the tax system to ensure that the wealthiest individuals and corporations pay a fair share. By ensuring that all citizens have equitable access to economic opportunities and political representation, it would be possible to counter the influence of the plutocratic elite and restore a sense of democratic integrity to the political system.

The rise of plutocratic oligarchy in the United States presents a grave challenge to the health of its democracy. The increasing concentration of wealth and power in the hands of a few individuals and corporations undermines the principles of equality and representation that are fundamental to the democratic system. Through mechanisms like corporate lobbying, campaign financing, and the revolving door between government and the private sector, the wealthy have been able to exert disproportionate influence over public policy, often to the detriment of broader societal interests. However, efforts to address these imbalances, such as campaign finance reform, increased transparency, and measures to reduce income inequality, offer a path forward to restore democratic integrity and ensure that the political system works for all citizens, not just the affluent few. Reducing the influence of money in politics and addressing the growing wealth gap are essential steps in creating a more equitable and just society, where the principles of democracy can flourish once again.[128-130]

THE INDISPENSABLE ROLE OF FREEDOM IN U.S. FOREIGN POLICY

Freedom has long been foundational to the identity of the United States; it is a concept that has shaped not just the domestic character but also the foreign policy of the U.S. Since the founding of the Republic, the United States has accepted the notion that its liberty and its self-determination were the cornerstones, not only of the country but of a new world order as well. This dedication to freedom is not just an issue of lofty ideals but is a matter of national security. The United States has long understood that liberty at home requires vigilance abroad, because peace, though a noble aspiration, cannot be secured without justice. That justice, the United States has long claimed, is best secured through strong support for democratic principles and strong opposition to the rise of authoritarianism—which has the potential to destabilize the international order and threaten the freedoms of all nations.

Right from the beginning, the Founding Fathers of the new nation understood that its survival would require more than local safety. And in the wake of the fledgling U.S. government stood powerful European empires hungry to expand their empires worldwide. The Founders understood that domestic freedom could not be an island—it was intimately connected to the balance of power abroad. Armed with this understanding, the first leaders of the Republic created policies that would permit the United States to form alliances, strengthen its defensive capacities, and exert an influence in international affairs. These policies would be imperative for the fledgling nation to survive, and it quickly became apparent that freedom and security were inseparable.

As these principles helped shape American foreign policy, the United States industrialized and grew more powerful. By the mid-20th century, the U.S. had transformed from a new, isolated country to a global superpower. After World War II, the United States became the primary architect of a new post-war order, taking the lead in rebuilding nations ravaged by the recent war and helping establish the United Nations and other international institutions to promote an international era of stability, freedom, and democracy. The U.S. became the chief upholder of democratic principles, trying to stem the onslaught of totalitarian ideals like communism, which had taken root in the Soviet Union and China. It was a time of ideological contention, where the United States emerged as the bastion of freedom against the forces of authoritarianism, with its mission of delivering democratic governance and personal freedoms around the globe.

The twenty-first century is different: New and complex challenges have dotted the global horizon, and authoritarian regimes have reemerged and evolved. These and other countries—Russia, China, Iran, and North Korea—replace one of the greatest threats to international stability: the way they employ all the tools, the peaceful less than violent, including the set of ideas and practices through which they want to subvert democratic practices and the rule of law that the United States has long promoted. These regimes wield a toolkit of tactics—economic coercion, military aggression, and disinformation campaigns—to undermine democracy in nations around the world, erode international institutions, and extend their own despotic agendas. For example, Russia has used cyberattacks and election interference to manipulate political processes in Western democracies, and China has used economic pressure and military posturing in the South China Sea and Taiwan to assert its dominance. In the meantime, North Korea and Iran have both attempted nuclear weapons programs, creating risks of regional strife and challenges to the global non-proliferation regime. These adversaries, most of whom espouse authoritarian ideologies, directly challenge the value of freedom and democracy that have been hallmarks of U.S. foreign policy.

American foreign policy in the twenty-first century should respond to the gradual transformation of the world order. Although the pursuit of peace remains paramount, peace will not be achieved through isolation or appeasement of authoritarian regimes. The United States must instead lead from the front, using strategic action to defend freedom and democracy from its enemies. That involves supporting international alliances and coalitions, standing resolutely in defense of democratic norms, and holding authoritarian regimes accountable for their actions. The new democratic environment will require technologists to develop effective new forms of warfare, such as cyber defense and economic sanctions, without expanding violent conflict, and take precautionary action to deter adversaries from undermining democratic institutions. It also means that the United States needs to cede human rights, the rule of law, and the expansion of democracy around the world as a calling card.

Moreover, the United States must confront emerging threats that blur traditional lines of security. Non-state actors, such as transnational terrorist organizations and extremist groups, remain a significant threat to global stability. These actors typically work across national borders, leveraging new technologies, including social media and encrypted communications, to attract and engage potential recruits. In meeting these threats, U.S. foreign policy needs to be nimble and collaborative—partnering with the international community to combat the spread of violent extremism and address the underlying conditions of instability.

The United States must also grapple with its relationship with ascendant world powers, especially China. China is increasingly seeking to position itself as a regional (indeed global) hegemon—while its authoritarian model represents an alternative to liberal democracy. The United States needs to establish a mechanism to engage China that encourages peaceful coexistence but protects its allies and the democratic way of life. This will necessitate a nuanced approach—part competition and part cooperation—on global issues like climate change, trade, and public health.

In the Middle East, the U.S. is faced with its messy geopolitical dynamics, as authoritarian regimes like Iran remain threats to regional stability. Iran cannot continue to be allowed to destabilize the Middle East by supporting proxy groups, developing nuclear capabilities, and conducting destabilizing operations in Syria, Iraq, and elsewhere in the world. The U.S. needs to ensure Iran never obtains nuclear arms, but also continue supporting the democratizing forces and seeking peace in the area.

The centrality of freedom to U.S. foreign policy is no less true today than it was at the nation's founding. But these foreign policy approaches were never exclusive to U.S. domestic politics; the prioritization of liberty and commitment to securing the world were both key themes undergirding U.S. foreign relations, especially in the early period of U.S. history, and were essential to understanding the United States' relationship to the world—including by informing the U.S.

foreign policy approach to security in the global environment. The context of international relations has evolved, yet the United States' commitment to defending democratic values, promoting human rights, and countering authoritarianism is essential for global stability and peace. In a world that is more complex and interconnected than ever before, American foreign policy must remain strategic and proactive—working to protect the freedoms that are the very foundation of our nation's identity and to ensure that the world is as free and secure as possible.

DEFENSIVE ALLIANCES AND GLOBAL STRATEGY

Defensive alliances like NATO and regional treaties such as SEATO have long been pillars of American foreign policy, providing critical frameworks for securing American interests and deterring potential adversaries. These alliances offer collective defense, pooling the military capabilities of member nations to create a formidable deterrent against external aggression. The very presence of these alliances demonstrates the collective strength of the participating countries, signaling to any would-be aggressors that they would face a united front in the event of conflict. NATO, for instance, has served as a cornerstone of transatlantic security since its creation in 1949, deterring aggression in Europe and maintaining stability in a region historically prone to conflict. Similarly, regional agreements like SEATO, though less active today, aimed to counter the spread of communism in Southeast Asia during the Cold War, providing a strategic counterbalance to communist forces in the region.

However, while these defensive alliances have been essential for maintaining security, they are not without limitations. One significant shortcoming is that they are inherently reactive, designed primarily to address direct military threats. These alliances offer protection to member states, but they do not extend beyond their established boundaries. This means that regions or countries outside the reach of these alliances remain vulnerable to aggression, destabilization, or coercion. For example, while NATO's security umbrella has kept Europe largely peaceful, regions in Africa, Asia, and the Middle East—outside NATO's purview—continue to experience instability, conflict, and the influence of adversarial powers. These gaps in coverage expose critical vulnerabilities that defensive alliances alone cannot address.

Furthermore, defensive alliances are often insufficient in countering more subtle forms of aggression, such as political subversion, which is increasingly favored by authoritarian regimes. Unlike overt military invasions, subversion operates through covert means—spreading disinformation, supporting proxy groups, manipulating political systems, or interfering in elections. These tactics are designed to undermine governments from within, destabilize societies, and weaken democratic institutions, all without triggering a military response that would activate defense treaties. Authoritarian powers, such as Russia and China, have become adept at leveraging these strategies, using cyberattacks, economic pressure, and influence operations to achieve their geopolitical objectives without resorting to conventional warfare. The use of political subversion and hybrid warfare represents a growing threat that defensive alliances are ill-equipped to address directly.

The historical examples of Cuba and Iraq illustrate the limitations of relying on purely defensive strategies in the face of such threats. In Cuba, the U.S. spent decades trying to contain the spread of communism through military and diplomatic means, yet it was the Cuban government's own reliance on Soviet-backed subversion tactics that posed the greatest challenge. While U.S. military power deterred direct Soviet intervention, it was the internal dynamics, exacerbated by economic hardship, ideological polarization, and external support, that created long-term instability on the island. Similarly, in Iraq, the U.S. military's intervention in 2003[131] was predicated on the idea of preventing the development of weapons of mass destruction. While the military campaign was a conventional success, the subsequent occupation and lack of strategic engagement with Iraq's civil society and political structures led to a power vacuum and the rise of extremist groups, contributing to years of instability and conflict.

To address the limitations of defensive alliances and better respond to the challenges posed by political subversion, the U.S. must adopt a more proactive approach to global security. Offensive strategies are necessary not only in terms of military engagement but also through the broader means of influence. One key element of this is fostering civil society in vulnerable regions. By promoting the development of strong, resilient civil institutions, the U.S. can help create societies better equipped to resist internal destabilization efforts. Civil society organizations, media, and grassroots movements play a crucial role in defending democratic values and resisting authoritarian encroachment. Supporting these entities, particularly in authoritarian-leaning or conflict-prone regions, can help counter the influence of foreign adversaries and promote long-term stability.

Another offensive strategy involves supporting dissident movements within authoritarian regimes. By providing resources, training, and a platform for voices of opposition, the U.S. can help nurture political alternatives that may one day challenge entrenched regimes. These efforts can range from supporting independent media and human rights organizations to offering asylum or financial aid to those targeted by oppressive governments. This is not merely about ideological promotion but about empowering local populations to take charge of their own futures and resist outside manipulation. The success of dissident movements often relies on external support, and the U.S. has historically played a role in facilitating such movements in places like Eastern Europe during the Cold War or more recently in the Middle East and Asia.

Economic tools also form a key part of the U.S. strategy to weaken authoritarian regimes from within. Economic sanctions targeting financial measures and trade restrictions can serve as leverage to press governments to alter their behavior. However, economic tools need to be applied strategically. Broad-based sanctions often harm the general population and can inadvertently bolster the regime by giving it a scapegoat to blame for economic woes. More effective are targeted sanctions that specifically address the wealth and assets of regime elites, preventing them from using their control of resources to maintain power. In addition, fostering trade and economic partnerships with democratic countries, while isolating authoritarian regimes from international financial systems, can further marginalize oppressive regimes and create incentives for internal reform.

While defensive alliances remain vital for protecting national and allied interests, they must be complemented by offensive strategies that address the full spectrum of threats facing global security today. The rise of authoritarianism, political subversion, and hybrid warfare requires the U.S. to think beyond traditional military deterrence and engage in proactive efforts to promote democratic values, empower civil society, and destabilize regimes from within. In this way, the U.S. can ensure a more robust, comprehensive approach to maintaining global stability and protecting freedom in the face of evolving threats.

FOREIGN AID: A TOOL FOR STABILITY AND INFLUENCE

Foreign aid has been a cornerstone of U.S. foreign policy for decades, serving both strategic and humanitarian objectives. The modern era of U.S. foreign assistance began with the **Marshall Plan** in 1948[132], which allocated over $13 billion to rebuild war-torn Europe after World War II. This initiative not only facilitated economic recovery but also aimed to counter the spread of communism by stabilizing allied nations.[133]

In 1961, President John F. Kennedy further institutionalized foreign aid by signing the **Foreign Assistance Act**, leading to the creation of the **U.S. Agency for International Development (USAID)**. This agency was tasked with administering economic and humanitarian assistance worldwide, reflecting the U.S. commitment to fostering global development and democracy.[134]

Throughout the Cold War, foreign aid remained a vital tool for the U.S., providing substantial support to countries like South Korea and Taiwan to bolster their economies and deter communist influence. This strategy underscored the role of aid in promoting political stability and aligning global partners with U.S. interests.[135]

In recent years, the U.S. has continued to allocate significant resources to foreign assistance. In 2023, nearly $65 billion was spent on various programs, including education, health services, military support, and humanitarian aid. These efforts not only address immediate global challenges but also serve to enhance U.S. national security by fostering international stability and goodwill.[136]

Despite fluctuations in public opinion and political leadership, foreign aid persists as a fundamental aspect of U.S. foreign policy, reflecting a blend of altruistic values and strategic interests.

Foreign aid has long been an essential component of U.S. foreign policy, serving as a powerful tool for fostering stability, promoting development, and enhancing American influence globally. It plays a particularly critical role in addressing the root causes of instability—issues like poverty, weak governance, and social discontent—which often serve as fertile ground for extremist ideologies and violent conflict. By addressing these underlying factors, foreign aid helps to reduce the appeal of radical movements, offering alternative paths to prosperity, peace, and security. In doing so, it enhances the security of both the recipient nations and the United States, ensuring that fragile regions are less likely to fall into turmoil and be less susceptible to the influence of adversaries.

One of the primary ways that foreign aid contributes to stability is through the promotion of economic development. In many parts of the world, poverty and lack of opportunity fuel frustration and disillusionment, which can lead to social unrest or the rise of extremist groups. By providing aid that focuses on building infrastructure, creating jobs, and fostering entrepreneurship, the United States can help create a foundation for long-term economic growth. This not only improves the living standards of individuals in these regions but also opens new markets for U.S. goods and services, creating mutually beneficial relationships. Furthermore, aid aimed at strengthening economies can help stabilize governments by ensuring that they can meet the needs of their populations, reducing the likelihood of political instability or collapse.

In addition to economic development, foreign aid is instrumental in enhancing governance and institutional capacity in fragile states. Weak governance is another key driver of instability, as ineffective or corrupt governments often fail to address the needs of their citizens or provide basic public services. This failure can create a power vacuum that is often filled by extremist groups or criminal organizations, further exacerbating instability. Through foreign aid programs that support governance reforms, the rule of law, and the development of strong institutions, the U.S. helps to build the capacity of local governments to serve their populations effectively. This strengthens the overall stability of the region and reduces the likelihood of conflict or the rise of authoritarian regimes.

Foreign aid also plays a critical role in enhancing the capacity of allied nations to address shared global threats. In an increasingly interconnected world, challenges such as terrorism, cyberattacks, and pandemics do not respect borders, and addressing them requires international cooperation. U.S. foreign aid enables allied nations to bolster their security forces, improve intelligence sharing, and develop critical infrastructure that can help counter these threats. For example, in regions like the Sahel, U.S. aid has been crucial in supporting counterterrorism efforts, providing training and equipment to local forces, and helping to prevent extremist groups from gaining control of large territories. This not only protects the stability of the region but also prevents these groups from using these areas as launching pads for attacks on Western interests or allies.

Public health is another area where foreign aid plays a significant role in promoting both stability and goodwill. The U.S. has a long history of responding to global health crises, and its assistance has often been vital in preventing the spread of diseases that could have global implications. A prime example of this was the U.S. response to the Ebola outbreak in West Africa. U.S. aid in the form of medical supplies, personnel, and logistical support helped to contain the spread of the virus, saving countless lives in the process. But beyond the immediate health impact, this assistance also helped to strengthen the U.S.'s reputation as a global leader in humanitarian efforts. In regions struggling with weak healthcare systems, this kind of aid fosters goodwill and lays the groundwork for deeper diplomatic and economic partnerships in the future. When countries see the U.S. taking action to protect their citizens' health, they are more likely to view the United States as a reliable partner and ally, creating a foundation for future cooperation on a range of issues.

Foreign aid is also essential in the realm of education, which is another critical pillar for fostering long-term stability and development. Education programs funded by the U.S. improve access to quality schooling in countries where the educational system may be underdeveloped or in need of reform. These programs not only help to equip young people with the skills needed to contribute to their economies but also promote values such as tolerance, civic participation, and democratic governance. By investing in education, the U.S.

helps to shape the next generation of leaders, who are more likely to support democratic principles and work toward peaceful solutions to conflict. In many cases, these education programs are also linked with broader efforts to empower women and marginalized groups, helping to create more inclusive societies.

One of the most strategic aspects of U.S. foreign aid is its ability to foster partnerships and alliances in regions that are crucial to American security and influence. When the U.S. provides aid to a country, it often strengthens its bilateral relationships, making those countries more inclined to cooperate on a range of issues, including military collaboration, intelligence sharing, and regional stability. This, in turn, enhances the U.S.'s ability to project power and influence globally. Foreign aid, therefore, serves not only as a tool for humanitarian assistance but also as an instrument of diplomacy and strategic partnership. By investing in the stability and development of key regions, the U.S. can maintain strong, positive relationships with important allies and ensure that American interests are well-represented in global decision-making.

Finally, the impact of U.S. foreign aid extends far beyond its immediate effects in recipient countries. The strategic use of aid can help to shape global order by promoting values such as democracy, human rights, and the rule of law. In a world where authoritarian regimes seek to expand their influence, U.S. foreign aid serves as a counterweight, helping to support countries that are striving to build open, democratic societies. Through its aid programs, the U.S. sends a clear message that it supports the aspirations of people around the world to live in freedom and peace. Whether through direct humanitarian assistance, health programs, or support for democratic governance, U.S. foreign aid strengthens the global fabric of stability, countering the influence of adversaries and contributing to a safer, more prosperous world.

In this way, foreign aid is not just an act of charity or altruism; it is an integral component of U.S. national security strategy. By addressing the root causes of instability and supporting the development of strong, democratic partners, the U.S. ensures that it remains a leader in promoting global peace, security, and prosperity.

MILITARY STRENGTH AND ECONOMIC RESILIENCE

Military strength remains a cornerstone of American power, essential not only for deterring potential aggressors but also for ensuring the nation's ability to respond swiftly and decisively to crises around the world. The presence of a formidable military force provides the U.S. with the leverage to influence global affairs, maintain stability in key regions, and safeguard its interests. However, military strength alone is insufficient to preserve America's leadership on the world stage. Economic resilience is equally crucial, as a strong and dynamic economy underpins not only the funding of defense initiatives but also the ability to project influence globally. A prosperous economy allows the U.S. to maintain a competitive edge in technological innovation, support the development of critical infrastructure, and invest in the capacity to respond to both military and non-military threats.

In particular, the U.S. must focus on reducing its vulnerabilities to coercion, especially those that arise from dependence on authoritarian regimes for essential resources. Historically, American reliance on foreign oil has made the nation susceptible to manipulation by countries with unstable or adversarial political agendas. To mitigate these risks, it is imperative that the U.S. transition away from an oil-dependent economy, focusing on alternative energy sources that not only promote sustainability but also enhance energy security. Investments in renewable energy, such as solar, wind, and hydrogen, as well as innovations in battery storage and smart grid technology, will reduce dependence on global energy markets controlled by hostile powers. These steps will not only diminish the leverage of authoritarian regimes but also help the U.S. lead the world in combating climate change, a global challenge that is intricately tied to national security.

Economic strength also plays a pivotal role in maintaining the U.S.'s strategic and technological edge. By ensuring continued investment in sectors such as artificial intelligence, cybersecurity, biotechnology, and advanced manufacturing, the U.S. can remain a leader in critical technologies that shape both military capabilities and broader geopolitical dynamics. These technologies enable the development of advanced defense systems, improve military readiness, and allow for innovation in areas like missile defense, autonomous systems, and cyber warfare. At the same time, a strong economy allows for investments in infrastructure that enhance national security. Modernizing ports, transportation networks, and communications systems ensures the U.S. can efficiently mobilize resources and respond to crises, while also securing supply chains that are vital to both civilian and military functions.

Alongside economic and technological strength, the U.S. must maintain the ability to engage in limited warfare, enabling it to address regional conflicts and stabilize volatile areas without escalating to the scale of full-scale wars. Limited warfare encompasses a variety of strategies and tactics that allow for targeted, flexible responses to threats without the need for massive mobilization of resources. The U.S. military must be equipped with advanced conventional forces capable of executing precision strikes, along with robust cyber capabilities that can disrupt enemy operations and protect U.S. interests in the digital domain. Cyber warfare is a growing domain of conflict that can have strategic implications far beyond traditional military engagements. Therefore, developing and refining capabilities in cyber defense and offense are critical to maintaining military readiness in an increasingly interconnected and digital world.

In addition to military and economic power, America's global leadership hinges on its ability to form and sustain strategic alliances. The U.S. should continue to work with like-minded nations to share the burden of defense, creating coalitions that can tackle regional challenges together. Through partnerships, whether formalized in treaties or ad hoc collaborations, the U.S. can extend its military reach and influence, while also promoting stability and security in critical regions. These alliances are particularly vital in areas where the U.S. cannot afford to be the sole actor. Multilateral efforts in counterterrorism, peacekeeping, disaster relief, and addressing regional tensions are just a few examples of how strategic alliances can amplify American military strength and diplomatic influence.

In summary, while military superiority is necessary for deterring aggression and securing national interests, it must be complemented by economic resilience to ensure that America remains a global leader. Reducing dependence on authoritarian-controlled resources, investing in emerging technologies, and maintaining the capability for limited warfare will enable the U.S. to address diverse threats effectively. A combination of military power, economic strength, and strategic alliances will ensure that America is well positioned to navigate the complexities of the modern world and maintain its leadership role in global affairs.

THREAT TO THE VOLUNTEER MILITARY

U.S. veterans should not depend on charities for healthcare, housing, food, education, or jobs.

The well-being of U.S. military veterans is integral to the strength and sustainability of the nation's volunteer military forces. Unfortunately, the poor treatment of veterans reflects a profound failure to honor the sacrifices made by those who have served the country. As the nation continues to depend on a volunteer military—where only three percent of Americans serve, and ninety percent of those volunteers sign up of their own volition[137]—the stakes are high. Veterans are not just symbols of national sacrifice but are also essential to the ongoing viability of military recruitment and retention. If veterans are neglected—if they are left to depend on charities for their healthcare, housing, food, education, or jobs—then this sends a clear and detrimental message to those still in active service. Veterans' dignity and well-being are crucial, not only for their own sense of fulfillment and honor but for the morale of active-duty personnel. When active-duty members see their predecessors suffer due to inadequate care and support, it can diminish their trust in the promises made to them after their service. This erosion of confidence can have a direct impact on recruitment, as prospective service members may be deterred by the idea that they, too, could be abandoned or under-supported once they retire from military service.

Moreover, the alarming statistic that eighteen veterans commit suicide every day[138] highlights the severity of the mental health crisis among former service members. The lack of sufficient mental healthcare, the lack of access to support systems, and the challenges of reintegration into civilian life all contribute to this devastating reality. If veterans are not provided with the necessary resources to transition smoothly into post-service life, they are left vulnerable to physical and mental hardships, which can have tragic outcomes. Addressing these issues is not just a moral obligation but a critical component of maintaining a strong and effective military force. The state of veterans' care directly impacts the effectiveness of the military as a whole; the strength of a military cannot solely rely on weapons and strategy but must also include the unwavering commitment of society to support and care for those who defend it.

Historically, the U.S. has made attempts to address the needs of its veterans through landmark initiatives such as the GI Bill. Signed into law in 1944,[139] the GI Bill was one of the most transformative pieces of legislation in American history. Its goal was to provide returning World War II veterans with the support needed to reintegrate into civilian life by offering benefits such as tuition assistance, home loans, and unemployment compensation. These benefits helped millions of veterans access higher education, leading to a better-educated workforce, increased homeownership, and a more robust middle class that contributed to the post-war economic boom. This initiative not only improved the lives of veterans but also served as a cornerstone of the nation's economic prosperity.

However, over the years, the benefits offered under the GI Bill have seen erosion due to a variety of factors. The original 1944 bill expired in 1956, and while subsequent iterations like the Montgomery GI Bill in 1984[140] and the Post-9/11 GI Bill[141] in 2008 expanded and updated provisions, they have often failed to keep pace with rising costs and the evolving needs of veterans. For instance, the Montgomery GI Bill required service members to contribute financially during their active-duty service, placing an initial burden on them despite the long-term promise of educational benefits. The Post 9/11 GI Bill, while broad in its coverage, has faced criticism for its administrative hurdles and occasional gaps in support, especially in cases involving nontraditional or private institutions. Additionally, the GI Bill's benefits have failed to match the rising costs of education and housing, which has made it more difficult for veterans to fully capitalize on the opportunities that the bill was intended to provide.

The decline in the purchasing power of GI Bill benefits, coupled with bureaucratic inefficiencies, has left many veterans struggling to afford the education and housing they were promised. The original intent of the GI Bill—to offer a pathway to economic mobility and stability for veterans—has been undermined by budgetary constraints and insufficient adjustments to account for modern economic realities.

The disparities between the benefits offered to veterans of different eras are another area of concern, creating a sense of inequity among service members who are unsure of whether the nation's commitment to them is truly enduring.

To ensure that the GI Bill remains a robust tool for supporting veterans, it is essential to address these gaps and streamline the benefits process. This means providing more flexibility in the use of benefits, increasing financial support to reflect current costs, and making the application process easier for veterans to navigate. By restoring the GI Bill to its full WWII potential, the U.S. can reinforce its commitment to the men and women who have served, while simultaneously strengthening the foundation of the military itself. Addressing the challenges facing veterans today is not only about fulfilling a moral duty; it is also about ensuring the future strength and readiness of the U.S. military by demonstrating that those who serve will be supported, honored, and cared for when their service ends.

DIPLOMATIC STRENGTH AND SOVEREIGNTY

Diplomacy plays a vital role in shaping U.S. foreign policy, acting as a bridge between national interests and international cooperation. While institutions like the United Nations offer platforms for dialogue, U.S. engagement must be firmly grounded in the protection and advancement of American values, sovereignty, and strategic objectives. A heavy reliance on multilateral organizations can sometimes weaken the effectiveness of American goals, particularly when those institutions fail to take decisive action in the face of global threats. This has been evident in past conflicts where UN resolutions proved insufficient in addressing immediate security challenges, leaving the U.S. to take a more direct approach.

In navigating global diplomacy, the U.S. must project confidence and steadfastness. This means consistently advocating for human rights, democratic principles, and the protection of sovereignty, particularly in regions where authoritarianism threatens to undermine global stability. U.S. diplomatic efforts should never be about appeasing adversaries but rather ensuring that American ideals are respected on the world stage. Nations may not always agree with or support American policies, but the U.S. must ensure that its strength and commitment to justice are undeniable. It is not through compromise on core values that global respect is earned but through resolute action, principled leadership, and a willingness to defend the rights of free peoples, both at home and abroad.

By maintaining a diplomatic approach rooted in strength and unwavering dedication to justice, the U.S. can foster a global environment where its sovereignty is respected and its interests are safeguarded, all while promoting peace, stability, and democratic values worldwide.

For the FUTURE OF AMERICAN DEMOCRACY (Conclusion)

As Theodore Roosevelt famously stated, "To announce that there must be no criticism of the President... is morally treasonable to the American public."

For Secular Government: Victory over Authoritarians

Fascism and plutocratic oligarchy are forms of authoritarianism that concentrate power in the hands of the few, suppressing democratic principles and eroding individual freedoms. Fascism centralizes control through nationalism, militarism, and often violent suppression of dissent, demanding loyalty to a single authority or ideology. Similarly, a plutocratic oligarchy consolidates political and economic power among a wealthy elite, manipulating laws and institutions to serve their interests at the expense of the broader population. Both systems undermine equality, transparency, and accountability, silencing opposition and restricting civic participation to maintain their dominance. In essence, they are authoritarian regimes that exploit different mechanisms—one through fear and ideology, the other through wealth and influence—but share the common goal of absolute control and the subjugation of the masses. Victory over authoritarianism—foreign and domestic—must be the guiding objective of all Americans. This requires a shift from reactive defense to proactive engagement. The erosion of accountability was not inevitable. It is a consequence of choices, and with collective will, those choices can be reversed.

Project 2025, with its potential to align policy with extreme ideologies, could accelerate these trends. The dangers lie not just in overt authoritarianism but in incremental changes that erode civil liberties and institutions over time. Historical parallels underscore the need for vigilance to ensure democratic resilience and prevent a resurgence of totalitarianism in any guise.

The Founding Fathers risked everything for the promise of freedom, knowing that liberty requires vigilance and sacrifice. Today, America faces a similar test. To preserve the ideals of democracy and justice, we must confront authoritarianism with courage and resolve. The risks are significant, but the alternative—a world dominated by oppression—is unacceptable. By leading with strength, compassion, and a clear vision, the United States can secure a future where peace and freedom prevail.

Authoritarianism threatens the very principles of freedom, equality, and justice that define democratic societies. It erodes rights, silences dissent and consolidates power in the hands of a few at the expense of the many. To safeguard democracy, we must act decisively and collectively. Here is how we achieve this vision:

1. **Protect Fundamental Rights**

    - **Defend Free Speech:** Advocate for protections against censorship and support independent journalism to ensure access to unbiased information.

    - **Stand for Justice:** Oppose discriminatory policies and practices that marginalize communities or violate civil liberties.

- **Uphold the Rule of Law:** Demand accountability and transparency from leaders to prevent abuses of power.

- **Ensure Checks and Balances:** Advocate for strong legislative and judicial oversight to counteract executive overreach.

2. **Mobilize Communities**

- **Educate and Engage:** Spread awareness about the dangers of authoritarianism and equip citizens with tools to recognize and resist it.

- **Support Activism:** Join or donate to organizations working to protect democracy and human rights.

- **Build Solidarity:** Unite across political, social, and cultural divides to form coalitions for shared democratic values.

3. **Resist the Spread of Misinformation**

- **Challenge Propaganda:** Fact-check and counter false narratives used to justify authoritarian actions.

- **Promote Media Literacy:** Teach others how to discern credible information from manipulative content.

- **Defend Truth:** Uphold the integrity of peer-reviewed science and restore public and post-secondary education to high standards of excellence and critical thinking.

For The Voter: Restoring Trust and Ensuring Equity in the U.S. Electoral System

The foundation of American democracy relies on the principle that every voice matters and every vote counts. Yet, systemic barriers, outdated practices, and undue influences undermine this promise.

Together, we must take bold and comprehensive action to protect voting rights, restore trust in elections, and create a more inclusive, equitable democratic process. Here is how we can achieve this vision:

1. **Safeguard Voting Rights and Accessibility**

    - Establish Election Day as a federal holiday to remove barriers for working citizens.

    - Expand early voting, mail-in ballot options, and polling resources to reach underserved communities

    - Demand that voter districts be drawn without regard to voter party affiliation to prevent manipulation that dilutes voter power.

2. **Strengthen Electoral Integrity**

    - Implement transparent voter ID systems and provide free standardized voter IDs.

    - Use independent, nonpartisan commissions to eliminate gerrymandering.

    - Enhance election security with clear auditing and fraud prevention measures.

3. **Combat Wealth and Foreign Influence in Campaigns**

    - Limit the influence of political action committees (PACs) and cap campaign contributions from corporations and restrict foreign entities.

    - Transition to publicly funded elections to ensure fair competition and prioritize the public interest.

4. **Modernize Electoral Processes**

   - Adopt ranked choice voting to reduce polarization and ensure majority support for elected officials.

   - Reform the Electoral College to reflect the will of the people through proportional allocation of electoral votes.

5. **Rebuild Trust in Elections**

   - Partner with social media platforms to counter misinformation and foreign interference.

   - Empower citizens through education about their rights in a democracy and dispel myths.

   - Reintroduce civics education in schools to empower future generations.

For Representation of Taxation: Prioritizing Government Spending

The principle of **"no taxation without representation"** remains essential in modern governance. Every dollar collected from taxpayers must reflect a commitment to their voices, needs, and aspirations. To ensure government spending prioritizes the well-being of all citizens, we must demand a system that values equity, accountability, and responsiveness.

1. **Demand Responsible Government Spending**

   - **Prioritize Essential Services:** Advocate for investments in healthcare, education, infrastructure, and housing that benefit the majority of citizens.

   - **Combat Waste and Corruption:** Insist on transparency and accountability to eliminate misuse of taxpayer funds.

- **Address Climate and Public Safety:** Support spending on sustainable energy, disaster preparedness, and national security to safeguard future generations.

2. **Push for Tax Equity**

- **Fair Taxation Policies:** Demand a progressive tax system that ensures the wealthiest contribute their fair share.

- **Eliminate Loopholes:** Close tax breaks and incentives that disproportionately benefit corporations and wealthy individuals.

- **Reduce Corporate Influence:** Cap campaign contributions and reduce the role of lobbying in shaping tax policy.

3. **Ensure Public Participation in Budget Decisions**

- **Increase Transparency:** Advocate for public access to government budgets and spending reports.

- **Encourage Citizen Input:** Push for participatory budgeting initiatives where communities help decide how local funds are allocated.

4. **Hold Leaders Accountable**

- **Track Spending Priorities:** Monitor whether elected officials' budgetary decisions align with campaign promises and public needs.

- **Vote for Accountability:** Support candidates who prioritize responsible taxation and fair representation.

**Representation matters. Accountability matters.
Demand a government that puts people first.**

For Civil Liberties: Equal Rights for ALL

The protection of **civil liberties** and the guarantee of **equal justice** are the cornerstones of a free and democratic society. Yet, these fundamental rights are under constant threat from policies and systems that disproportionately target marginalized communities. We must act now to safeguard these rights for every individual, regardless of race, gender, sexual orientation, or socioeconomic status.

1. **Stand Against Systemic Inequality**

   - **End Racial Discrimination:** Advocate for comprehensive police reform, an end to mass incarceration, and the dismantling of discriminatory laws that disproportionately impact communities of color.

   - **Fight for Equal Rights:** Demand full legal equality for all people, regardless of gender, race, religion, or sexual identity. Challenge laws and practices that perpetuate discrimination.

2. **Protect Fundamental Freedoms**

   - **Safeguard Free Speech and Assembly:** Defend the right to free expression, peaceful protest, and the ability to criticize the government without fear of retribution.

   - **Support Privacy Rights:** Push for stronger protections against government surveillance, ensuring that individuals' personal freedoms and privacy are respected.

3. **Demand Equal Access to Justice**

   - **Ensure Fair Trials:** Advocate for an end to biased practices in the legal system, ensuring that everyone receives a fair trial, legal representation, and equal treatment under the law.

- **Reform the Justice System:** Call for an end to mass incarceration, the criminalization of poverty, and the abolition of practices that disproportionately harm marginalized communities, such as cash bail.

4. **Champion Civil Rights Legislation**

- **Enforce Anti-Discrimination Laws:** Push for stronger enforcement of existing civil rights laws and advocate for new legislation that protects individuals from discrimination in housing, employment, education, and public accommodations.

- **Expand Voting Rights:** Protect and expand voting rights to ensure that every citizen, regardless of background, can participate in the democratic process.

- **Support Justice-Driven Candidates:** Vote for leaders committed to civil rights, criminal justice reform, and policies that uphold equal protection under the law.

The Courage to Reclaim the Republic Through Vigilance

"…we must never compromise the cause of America, the cause of all mankind. Our great nation should ever diligently remain the shining example of human rights and provide international leadership and hope for Freedom. It is for this fact alone that we must remain a United Nation." Barry Goldwater

These solutions are neither easy nor quick. They demand courage, compromise, and a willingness to prioritize long-term national well-being over short-term partisan gain. History shows that when people come together with a shared purpose, even seemingly insurmountable challenges can be overcome.

As Ben Franklin warned, we have a republic—if we can keep it. The responsibility now falls to this generation to rise above division, reject cynicism, and reclaim the ideals that have always defined the American experiment: liberty, equality, and justice for all.

For many years, the principal domestic threat to our freedom seemed rooted in the doctrines of communism and authoritarian regimes. Today, however, this no longer appears to be the main danger. A century ago, the nation faced a comparable menace: the concentration of economic power. Large corporations, wielding monopoly control over entire industries, undermined the competitive forces essential to freedom. In response, we enacted antitrust legislation like the Sherman Act to curb such abuses. Yet history, when left unchecked, has a way of repeating itself.

For the People. The task ahead is monumental but not impossible. To address these systemic issues, we must revisit the founding principles of the republic and adapt them to the challenges of the twenty-first century. This begins with a commitment to reforms that prioritize the public good over special interests.

The American Revolution was not merely a war for independence; it was a rebellion against unaccountable power and systemic exploitation. The grievances against the British monarchy—taxation without representation, property seizures, and laws crafted to benefit elites—resonate today, albeit in more nuanced and institutionalized forms. Despite the democratic framework built by the Constitution, many of the abuses the colonists fought against have re-emerged within the very system designed to prevent them.

Modern governance is plagued by similar dynamics: legislative processes often cater to a narrow, powerful elite, while the average citizen struggles to have their voice heard. Lobbyists and special interest groups dominate policymaking, while the public watches in frustration as laws are passed that seem detached from the needs of the majority. These parallels highlight how the erosion of accountability is not just a failure of institutions; it is a betrayal of the principles on which the nation was founded.

In modern times, oligarchs—both in the United States and other industrialized nations—have exploited free enterprise to consolidate wealth and influence. Massive productivity gains and concentrated wealth have quelled the social conditions that might otherwise provoke class struggle. Rather than challenging this imbalance, the masses often idolize billionaire oligarchs, embracing their authoritarian ideologies.

We must wage a new war on all forms of monopolistic and oligarchic power—whether corporate or individual wealth based. The true enemy of freedom is unchecked power, and freedom's defenders must combat its concentration wherever it arises.

For the Voter. Social media has become the dominant force shaping our culture and consciousness, particularly for younger generations. While much attention is given to how these platforms can be harnessed—whether to educate, inform, or influence—there is far less focus on how education might empower individuals to critically engage with them. This imbalance leaves users vulnerable to manipulation, misinformation, and a shallow, passive engagement with the world.

Aldous Huxley's warnings in *Brave New World*[142] resonate powerfully in this context. He cautioned that the true danger to society lay not in overt oppression but in distraction—a world where people are so consumed by entertainment and surface-level content that they lose the ability to think critically or question authority. The problem is not just that people laugh instead of think, but that they no longer understand why they are laughing or what deeper truths they are missing. Social media has created a similar dynamic, inundating users with fleeting, curated information that prioritizes engagement over substance.

To counter this, education must take on the critical task of teaching students not only how to use social media but also how to question its motives, biases, and impacts. This is not merely about media literacy; it is about understanding the politics and epistemology of platforms that shape our perceptions and choices. Schools must place this critical engagement at the core of their mission, equipping students to recognize the forces influencing their thoughts and behaviors.

As Huxley suggested, we are in a race between education and disaster. If we fail to educate young people to think critically about social media, we risk a future where distraction replaces meaningful engagement and where control is exerted not through force but through passive compliance. Education must empower individuals to reclaim agency in the digital age, ensuring that technology serves humanity rather than undermines it.

Politicians receive massive campaign donations from special interests seeking to influence legislation. In return, these lawmakers often enact policies that serve these interests—even when they harm voters.

The lack of transparency in our political system enables this cycle. Current disclosure laws are outdated and ineffective: Many donations go unreported for months, while some are never disclosed electronically, making it difficult for citizens and journalists to "follow the money."

Dark money floods elections, funneled through groups with secret donors who spend vast sums to influence outcomes. These groups exploit loopholes to make unlimited contributions and run ads to elect or defeat candidates, all while hiding their funding sources.

Politicians also manipulate electoral maps, drawing district lines to secure their re-election and give their party an unfair advantage. This practice undermines fair representation and weakens voter power.

Running for office is prohibitively expensive, meaning most Americans cannot afford to contribute. This makes politicians reliant on a tiny fraction of wealthy donors and special interests, further skewing the system against ordinary voters.

The Citizens United ruling unleashed a wave of unchecked spending, allowing super PACs to spend unlimited funds to influence elections. Despite supposed restrictions against direct coordination with campaigns, these boundaries are regularly blurred, mocking the Supreme Court's mandate of independence.

Meanwhile, the definition of "lobbyist" is outdated, allowing many influencers, including former politicians and staff, to evade registration and disclosure requirements.

Even existing anti-corruption rules are weakly enforced. Agencies face partisan deadlocks and lack the tools to hold violators accountable, creating a system in which even lax rules can be broken with impunity.

A turning point will come when we entrust our affairs to leaders who recognize that their foremost duty is to relinquish the very power entrusted to them. This will happen when Americans across the nation elect public servants committed to upholding the Constitution and restoring the Republic—not self-proclaimed "leaders" who dictate what they believe is best for their constituents. True governance serves the people, empowering them to pursue happiness.

For Secular Government. History teaches us that authoritarianism often emerges under the guise of reform, order, or moral renewal. The parallels between the rise of the "Fourth Reich" and the ideological trajectory of Project 2025 serve as a stark warning. To protect democratic principles, it is essential to recognize and resist these patterns, safeguarding institutions, civil liberties, and the pluralistic values that underpin a free society. Ignoring these lessons risks repeating history's darkest chapters, with devastating consequences for democracy and human rights.

For Representation of Taxation. When a government prioritizes meeting the basic needs of its citizens—such as health, education, and safety—it cultivates a more productive workforce. Countries like Norway, Australia, Denmark, Sweden, and Canada, which consistently rank highest in GDP per capita[143] according to the World Bank, provide universally accessible public services, including healthcare, childcare, and workers' compensation. These investments foster economic growth by enhancing productivity, which, in turn, generates the tax revenue needed to sustain such services.

This is basic common sense. Capitalism thrives on transactions, and a robust, transaction-driven economy depends on policies that empower the people. It is the government's charge to safeguard this fertile economic environment by creating policies that serve the public good.

Demand that your tax dollars work for you and your community. Contact your representatives, join local budget advocacy groups, and educate others about the importance of equitable government spending. Together, we can build a system where taxation truly serves the people, ensuring fairness, opportunity, and progress for all.

For Civil Liberties for ALL. Defending civil liberties is essential to safeguarding the core principles of freedom, justice, and equality that form the foundation of a democratic society. Civil liberties protect individuals from unjust government interference, ensuring the rights to free speech, privacy, due process, and peaceful assembly. When these freedoms are eroded, authoritarianism and inequality take root, silencing marginalized voices and undermining accountability. History shows that once liberties are lost, regaining them is far more difficult and costly. We must act now to preserve these rights for ourselves and future generations, demanding transparent governance, fair legal systems, and equal justice for all. Defending civil liberties is not just a legal obligation but a moral imperative that defines who we are as a people. The time to defend our civil liberties and ensure equal justice for all is now.

Call to Action. These solutions are neither revolutionary nor unattainable. They are rooted in the principles articulated by the framers of the Constitution and echoed by historical leaders who have guided the nation through its greatest challenges. As Franklin D. Roosevelt once said, "The only thing we have to fear is fear itself." It is fear—fear of change, fear of the other—that often prevents us from pursuing bold solutions.

The responsibility for change lies with us, the people. As citizens, we must demand better from our leaders and from ourselves. We must reject the politics of division and instead embrace the principles of justice, equity, and accountability. Only by doing so can we fulfill the promise of the American experiment and ensure that the government truly serves the people.

I hope you have noticed that this book cites many references to support these beliefs. I am not concerned with converting anyone to a certain way of thinking. However, some will find that these beliefs resonate with them. These are the people who will provide the critical mass to begin the organization of the unvoiced majority to reclaim our republic.

Reclaiming our Republic starts with you. Speak out, organize, and demand action from your elected officials. Contact your representatives, attend protests, vote in every election, and hold those in power accountable. By standing together, we can protect democracy, uphold justice, and ensure that freedom prevails for generations to come. Together, we can build a society where justice is not a privilege for some but a right for all. **YOUR voice matters.**

Fight for fairness.
Fight for equality.
Fight for freedom.

Notes

1. McEvers, K. (n.d.). *What Mitch McConnell's early political days say about the Senate majority leader.* https://www.capradio.org/news/npr/story?story-id=747041518

2. *Abraham Lincoln's annual message to Congress—Concluding remarks. (n.d.).* https://www.abrahamlincolnonline.org/lincoln/speeches/congress.htm

3. *Henry Ford: Assembly Line—The Henry Ford. (n.d.).* https://www.thehenryford.org/collections-and-research/digital-collections/expert-sets/7139/

4. *Ford's Five-Dollar Day | The Henry Ford—Blog—The Henry Ford. (n.d.).* https://www.thehenryford.org/explore/blog/fords-five-dollar-day/

5. Roundtable, P. (2023, January). *Milton Hershey.* https://www.philanthropy-roundtable.org/hall-of-fame/milton-hershey/

6. *The Hershey Story | Family Attraction & Interactive Museum in Hershey, PA. (2025, January).* https://hersheystory.org/

7. contributors, W. (2024, November). *Milton S. Hershey.* https://en.wikipedia.org/wiki/Milton_S._Hershey

8. Company, T. B. (2024, September). *Environmental stewardship—Biltmore.* https://www.biltmore.com/our-story/our-mission/environmental-stewardship/

9. Perishable. (2016, August). *Our Legacy of Stewardship – Biltmore Farms, LLC Asheville NC.* https://www.biltmorefarms.com/community-development/legacy-of-stewardship/

10. contributors, W. (2025, January). *Biltmore Estate.* https://en.wikipedia.org/wiki/Biltmore_Estate

11. Goldwater, B. M., & Kennedy, R. F. (2007). *The Conscience of a Conservative.* Princeton University Press; JSTOR. https://doi.org/10.2307/j.ctv1jk0jvb

12. *Leviathan | Project Gutenberg. (n.d.).* https://www.gutenberg.org/files/3207/3207-h/3207-h.htm

13. *The Avalon Project: Federalist No 51. (n.d.).* https://avalon.law.yale.edu/18th_century/fed51.asp

14. *Research page: Lord Acton Quote Archive. (2025, February).* https://www.acton.org/research/lord-acton-quote-archive

15. *55 Corporations Paid $0 in Federal Taxes on 2020 Profits. (n.d.).* ITEP. Retrieved March 25, 2025, from https://itep.org/55-profitable-corporations-zero-corporate-tax/

16. *Group: 55 major firms did not pay any federal taxes last year—Baltimore Sun. (n.d.).* https://digitaledition.baltimoresun.com/tribune/article_popover.aspx?guid=ebe65dc6-53fd-4c80-95f4-f5b5897a09fb&utm_source=chatgpt.com

17. Gilens, M., & Page, B. I. (2014). Testing Theories of American Politics: Elites, Interest Groups, and Average Citizens. *Perspectives on Politics,* 12(3), 564–581. Cambridge Core. https://doi.org/10.1017/S1537592714001595

18. Zuesse, E. (2014, April). *The contradictions of the American electorate—CounterPunch.org.* https://www.counterpunch.org/2014/04/15/the-contradictions-of-the-american-electorate/

19. Citizens United v. FEC–FEC.gov. (n.d.). https://www.fec.gov/legal-resources/court-cases/citizens-united-v-fec/

20. McCoy, J., & Press, B. (n.d.). *What happens when democracies become perniciously polarized?* https://carnegieendowment.org/research/2022/01/what-happens-when-democracies-become-perniciously-polarized?lang=en

21. Kallmer, B. (2024, January). *Polarization versus Democracy | Journal of Democracy.* https://www.journalofdemocracy.org/articles/polarization-versus-democracy/

22. *NASCAR tracks get part of a nice little $70 million perk in the fiscal cliff deal* [updated]. (2013, January 2). Yahoo Sports. http://sports.yahoo.com/blogs/nascar-from-the-marbles/nascar-gets-nice-little-70-million-perk-fiscal-203238580--nascar.html

23. *Senator Warren Outlines How Bank Deregulation Bill Poses Risk to Economy | U.S. Senator Elizabeth Warren of Massachusetts. (n.d.).* Retrieved March 25, 2025, from https://www.warren.senate.gov/newsroom/press-releases/senator-warren-outlines-how-bank-deregulation-bill-poses-risk-to-economy

24. Mierjeski, A., Joshua KaplanJustin Elliott. (2024). *Clarence Thomas secretly accepted luxury trips from GOP donor.* https://www.propublica.org/article/clarence-thomas-scotus-undisclosed-luxury-travel-gifts-crow

25. Christenson, J., King, R., & Glebova, D. (2024). *Harris and Trump hit whopping $2.5B in campaign, PAC fundraising—But don't break 2020 records.* https://nypost.com/2024/10/28/us-news/harris-and-trump-hit-2-5b-in-campaign-pac-fundraising-but-dont-break-2020-records/

26. *U.S. Presidents: Number of executive orders signed 1789-2025. (n.d.).* Statista. Retrieved March 25, 2025, from https://www.statista.com/statistics/1125024/us-presidents-executive-orders/

27. *Executive Orders.* (n.d.). Federal Register. Retrieved March 25, 2025, from https://www.federalregister.gov/presidential-documents/executive-orders?utm_source=chatgpt.com

28. *How many executive orders has each president signed?* (n.d.). USAFacts. Retrieved March 25, 2025, from https://usafacts.org/articles/how-many-executive-orders-has-each-president-signed/

29. *Executive Orders Disposition Tables Historical Index.* (2024, June 6). National Archives. https://www.archives.gov/federal-register/executive-orders/disposition

30. National Constitution Center. (n). *Benjamin Franklin Closing Speech at the Constitutional Convention. National Constitution Center.* https://constitutioncenter.org/the-constitution/historic-document-library/detail/benjamin-franklin-closing-speech-at-the-constitutional-convention

31. *Eternal vigilance.* (2010, September). https://www.monticello.org/exhibits-events/blog/eternal-vigilance/

32. Garceau, O. (1956). *A Democrat Looks at His Party.* By Dean Acheson. (New York: Harper and Brothers. 1955. Pp. 199.). American Political Science Review, 50(3), 867–869. Cambridge Core. https://doi.org/10.2307/1951570

33. *A Republican looks at his party: Larson, Arthur: Free Download, Borrow, and Streaming: Internet Archive.* (1956). https://archive.org/details/republicanlooksa00lars/page/n5/mode/2up

34. Lopez, A. (2024, October 11). *How we know voter fraud is very rare in U.S. elections. NPR.* https://www.npr.org/2024/10/11/nx-s1-5147732/voter-fraud-explainer

35. *The myth of voter fraud.* (2024, October). https://www.brennancenter.org/issues/ensure-every-american-can-vote/vote-suppression/myth-voter-fraud

36. *Pennsylvania to spend $10 million on new voter registration system | AP News.* (n.d.). Retrieved March 25, 2025, from https://apnews.com/article/pennsylvania-voting-system-ff7feef816c4fccaed8f63d6ef616420

37. Williams, L. (2025, March 21). *Opinion: CT should take next step on ranked choice voting.* CT Insider. https://www.ctinsider.com/opinion/article/ranked-choice-voting-ct-20231668.php

38. *New Hampshire elections offer preview of citizenship voting rules | AP News.* (n.d.). Retrieved March 25, 2025, from https://apnews.com/article/save-act-voting-proof-citizenship-new-hampshire-5105986c3fc354d-3d61ec3480b49c788

39. *Michigan GOP lawmakers petition Supreme Court over MI election laws.* (n.d.). Retrieved March 25, 2025, from https://www.ourmidland.com/news/article/michigan-gop-supreme-court-election-laws-20239907.php?utm_source=chatgpt.com

40. *Georgia Supreme Court considers whether judge was right to block new election rules | AP News.* (n.d.). Retrieved March 25, 2025, from https://apnews.com/article/georgia-state-election-board-rules-supreme-court-8ff13f07f-d5a1869e5e8b72d3870316a

41. Layne, N., Tanfani, J., & Parker, N. (2024, October 31). *In U.S. swing states, officials brace for conspiracy theories and violence. Reuters.* https://www.reuters.com/world/us/us-swing-states-officials-brace-conspiracy-theories-violence-2024-10-30/

42. Mendoza, M. (2024, October 30). *Accessible voting options for Texas voters with disabilities. Axios.* https://www.axios.com/local/san-antonio/2024/10/30/texas-voting-disabilites-2024-election-options-curbside

43. Hise, R., & Lewis, D. (2019, March 25). *We Drew Congressional Maps for Partisan Advantage. That Was the Point. The Atlantic.* https://www.theatlantic.com/ideas/archive/2019/03/ralph-hise-and-david-lewis-nc-gerrymandering/585619/

44. *Maryland's 6th congressional district.* (2025). In Wikipedia. https://en.wikipedia.org/w/index.php?title=Maryland%27s_6th_congressional_district&oldid=1281957545

45. *Citizens United v. FEC.* (2025). In *Wikipedia.* https://en.wikipedia.org/w/index.php?title=Citizens_United_v._FEC&oldid=1279831476

46. Teachout, Z. (2014). *Corruption in America: From Benjamin Franklin's snuff box to Citizens United.* Harvard University Press.

47. Zephyr Teachout. (2025). In *Wikipedia.* https://en.wikipedia.org/w/index.php?title=Zephyr_Teachout&oldid=1275400188

48. Balcerzak, A. (2018, May 10). *Study: Most Americans want to kill 'Citizens United' with constitutional amendment.* Center for Public Integrity. http://publicintegrity.org/politics/study-most-americans-want-to-kill-citizens-united-with-constitutional-amendment/

49. The Ch. (n.d.). *Philanthropists' Political Donations in the 2024 Elections.*

50. West, D. M., & Nelson, K. (2024). *Foreign influence operations in the 2024 elections.* https://www.brookings.edu/articles/foreign-influence-operations-in-the-2024-elections/

51. McQue, K. (2025). *China tops list of countries trying to silence exiled dissidents*

over past decade, study shows. https://www.theguardian.com/global-development/2025/feb/12/quarter-countries-exiled-dissidents-china-governments-transnational-repression

52. *Ranked choice voting.* (n.d.). https://campaignlegal.org/democracyu/accountability/ranked-choice-voting

53. History.com Editors. (2020). *The Founding Fathers and the Electoral College.* History.com. https://www.history.com/news/electoral-college-founding-fathers-constitutional-convention

54. *The Electoral College and our broken presidential election system; Ash Center.* (2025, January). https://ash.harvard.edu/articles/the-electoral-college-and-our-broken-presidential-election-system/

55. *FairVote. (n). Problems with the Electoral College.* FairVote. https://archive3.fairvote.org/reforms/national-popular-vote/the-electoral-college/problems-with-the-electoral-college/

56. History.com Editors. (2020). *U.S. Presidents Who Won Without the Popular Vote.* History.com. https://www.history.com/news/presidents-electoral-college-popular-vote

57. New-York Historical Society. (n). *The Evolution of the Electoral College.* New-York Historical Society. https://www.nyhistory.org/blogs/the-evolution-of-the-electoral-college

58. *The National Popular Vote, explained.* (2022, October). https://www.brennancenter.org/our-work/research-reports/national-popular-vote-explained

59. Wallenfeldt & Jeff. (2025, February). *The Troubles | Summary, Causes, & Facts.* https://www.britannica.com/event/The-Troubles-Northern-Ireland-history

60. Naghshbandi, N. (2024). "The boot on my neck." https://www.hrw.org/report/2024/04/01/boot-my-neck/iranian-authorities-crime-persecution-against-bahais-iran

61. Ochsenwald, L, W., Kingston, & Paul. (2025, January). *Lebanese Civil War | Summary, History, Casualties, & Religious factions.* https://www.britannica.com/event/Lebanese-Civil-War

62. Lempinen, E. (2022, November). *The tortures of the Spanish Inquisition hold dark lessons for our time—Berkeley News.* https://news.berkeley.edu/2022/07/20/the-tortures-of-the-spanish-inquisition-hold-dark-lessons-for-our-time/

63. *Religion in Colonial America: Trends, regulations, and beliefs.* (2016, March). https://www.facinghistory.org/resource-library/religion-colonial-america-trends-regulations-beliefs

64. *Congressional record: United States. Congress: Free Download, Borrow, and Streaming: Internet Archive.* (1873). https://archive.org/details/congressionalrec127funit

65. United States Congress. (1981). *Congressional Record—Extensions of Remarks* (September 15, 1981). U.S. Government Publishing Office. https://www.congress.gov/bound-congressional-record/1981/09/15/127/extensions-of-remarks-section

66. Reid, T. R. (2023). *Republicans Rue Mecham's Return.* https://www.washingtonpost.com/archive/politics/1989/03/14/republicans-rue-mechams-return/4aef71ec-b626-444d-8e15-5a6dae85712c/

67. Goldberg, M. (2006). *Kingdom coming: The rise of Christian nationalism.* W. W. Norton.

68. Diamond, S. (1995). *Roads to dominion: Right-wing movements and political power in the United States.* Guilford Press.

69. Stewart, K. (2019). *The power worshippers: Inside the dangerous rise of religious nationalism.* Bloomsbury Publishing.

70. Edwards, L. (2013). *The Heritage Foundation at 40.* The Heritage Foundation. https://www.heritage.org/conservatism/commentary/the-heritage-foundation-40

71. Williams, D. K. (2010). *God's own party: The making of the Christian Right.* Oxford University Press.

72. Wikiquote. (n.d.). *Paul Weyrich.* https://en.wikiquote.org/wiki/Paul_Weyrich

73. Meagher, R. (2009, June). *Remembering the new right.* https://politicalresearch.org/2009/06/10/remembering-the-new-right-political-strategy-and-the-building-of-the-gop-coalition

74. History.com Editors. (2018). *The Infamous Willie Horton Ad.* History.com. https://www.history.com/news/george-bush-willie-horton-racist-ad

75. Heatherly, C. L., & Heritage Foundation (Washington, D. C.). (1981). *Mandate for leadership: Policy management in a conservative administration.* Heritage Foundation; WorldCat.

76. contributors, W. (2025, February). *Contract with America.* https://en.wikipedia.org/wiki/Contract_with_America

77. *A Timeline of Heritage successes | The Heritage Foundation.* (n.d.). https://www.heritage.org/article/timeline-heritage-successes

78. Chretien, S. (n.d.). *Project 2025 | The Heritage Foundation.* https://www.heritage.org/conservatism/commentary/project-2025

79. *Quotations from the speeches and other works of Theodore Roosevelt—Theodore*

Roosevelt Association. (n.d.). https://www.theodoreroosevelt.org/content. aspx?club_id=991271&module_id=339333&page_id=22

80. *Fears of a fourth Reich.* (n.d.). https://www.historytoday.com/archive/history-matters/fears-fourth-reich

81. *Project 2025 – A Threat to Public Health.* (n.d.). Retrieved March 25, 2025, from https://www.apha.org/topics-and-issues/public-health-under-threat/project-2025

82. Maslow, A. H. (1954). *Motivation and personality* (pp. xiv, 411). Harpers.

83. *Interpretation: The Sixteenth Amendment | Constitution Center.* (n.d.). https://constitutioncenter.org/the-constitution/amendments/amendment-xvi/interpretations/139

84. contributors, W. (2025, February). *History of taxation in the United States.* https://en.wikipedia.org/wiki/History_of_taxation_in_the_United_States

85. Levy & Michael. (2023, April). *Underwood-Simmons Tariff Act | 1913, Importance, & Purpose.* https://www.britannica.com/event/Underwood-Simmons-Tariff-Act

86. *Britannica money.* (n.d.). https://www.britannica.com/money/flat-tax

87. *Tax Complexity Now Costs the U.S. Economy Over $546 Billion Annually.* (2024, August 6). Tax Foundation. https://taxfoundation.org/data/all/federal/irs-tax-compliance-costs/

88. Barnes, M. (n.d.). *Classics in the History of Psychology – A. H. Maslow (1943) A Theory of Human Motivation.* https://psychclassics.yorku.ca/Maslow/motivation.htm

89. *The Great Experiment: George Washington and the American Republic.* (2013, May). https://www.themorgan.org/exhibitions/the-great-experiment

90. Barry Goldwater. (1994, July 13). *Job Protection For Gays. University of North Texas Libraries, UNT Digital Library.* https://digital.library.unt.edu/ark:/67531/metadc804553/

91. *Remarks at a Kennedy-Lawrence dinner in Pittsburgh, Pennsylvania | The American Presidency Project.* (n.d.). https://www.presidency.ucsb.edu/documents/remarks-kennedy-lawrence-dinner-pittsburgh-pennsylvania

92. *14th Amendment to the U.S. Constitution: Civil Rights (1868).* (2024, March). https://www.archives.gov/milestone-documents/14th-amendment

93. Civil Rights Act of 1866, "An Act to protect all Persons in the United States in their Civil Rights, and furnish the Means of their Vindication." (n.d.). https://constitutioncenter.org/the-constitution/historic-document-li-

brary/detail/civil-rights-act-of-1866-april-9-1866-an-act-to-protect-all-persons-in-the-united-states-in-their-civil-rights-and-furnish-the-means-of-their-vindication

94. USA PATRIOT Act of 2001 (2001). https://www.congress.gov/bill/107th-congress/house-bill/3162/text

95. *Politician Trading: If You Can't Stop Them, Join Them | Alerts and Articles | Insights | Ballard Spahr.* (n.d.). Retrieved March 25, 2025, from https://www.ballardspahr.com/insights/alerts-and-articles/2024/10/politician-trading-if-you-cant-stop-them-join-them?utm_source=chatgpt.com

96. *SEC.gov | Martha Stewart and Peter Bacanovic.* (n.d.). Retrieved March 25, 2025, from https://www.sec.gov/enforcement-litigation/litigation-releases/lr-19794?utm_source=chatgpt.com

97. *S.2038—STOCK Act | NIH Ethics Program.* (n.d.). Retrieved March 25, 2025, from https://ethics.od.nih.gov/STOCK-Act-S2038?utm_source=chatgpt.com

98. *The STOCK Act: The Failed Effort to Stop Insider Trading in Congress.* (n.d.). Campaign Legal Center. Retrieved March 25, 2025, from https://campaignlegal.org/update/stock-act-failed-effort-stop-insider-trading-congress

99. *How did the founding fathers view education?—U.S. constitution.net.* (2024, June). https://www.usconstitution.net/founding-fathers-on-education/

100. Warren, E. & Supreme Court of the United States. (1953). *U.S. Reports: Brown v. Board of Education, 347 U.S. 483.* Library of Congress. https://www.loc.gov/item/usrep347483/

101. Congress, U. S. (1958). *National Defense Education Act of 1958.* https://www.govinfo.gov/content/pkg/STATUTE-72/pdf/STATUTE-72-Pg1580.pdf

102. Gouinlock, & S, J. (2025, February). *John Dewey | Biography, Philosophy, Pragmatism, & Education.* https://www.britannica.com/biography/John-Dewey

103. Los Angeles Times. (1994). Barry Goldwater's Views on Abortion and the Religious Right. *Los Angeles Times.* https://www.latimes.com/archives/la-xpm-1994-07-28-me-20611-story.html

104. Congress, U. S. (2010). *Patient Protection and Affordable Care Act.* https://www.congress.gov/bill/111th-congress/house-bill/3590

105. Mott, L., & Stanton, E. C. (1848). *Report of the Woman's Rights Convention held at Seneca Falls, N.Y., July 19th and 20th, 1848.* https://www.nps.gov/

wori/learn/historyculture/report-of-the-womans-rights-convention.htm

106. States, U. (1920). *19th Amendment to the U.S. Constitution: Women's Right to Vote.* https://www.archives.gov/milestone-documents/19th-amendment

107. States, U. (1963). *Equal Pay Act of 1963.* https://www.dol.gov/agencies/whd/equal-pay-act

108. States, U. (1974). *Equal Credit Opportunity Act of 1974.* https://www.consumerfinance.gov/compliance/compliance-resources/other-applicable-requirements/equal-credit-opportunity-act/

109. States, U. (1972). *Title IX of the Education Amendments Act of 1972.* https://www2.ed.gov/about/offices/list/ocr/docs/tix_dis.html

110. Roe v. Wade (1973). https://www.oyez.org/cases/1971/70-18

111. Burke, T. (2006). *Me Too Movement.* https://www.loc.gov/item/lcwaN0025442/

112. VI, A. (1493). *Inter caetera.* https://www.gilderlehrman.org/history-resources/spotlight-primary-source/doctrine-discovery-1493

113. States, U. (1865). *Mississippi Black Code of 1865.* https://constitutioncenter.org/the-constitution/historic-document-library/detail/mississippi-south-carolina-black-codes-1865

114. *Jim Crow and Segregation | Classroom materials at the Library of Congress |* Library of Congress. (n.d.). https://www.loc.gov/classroom-materials/jim-crow-segregation/

115. United States. (1882). *Chinese Exclusion Act.* https://avalon.law.yale.edu/19th_century/chinese_exclusion_act.asp

116. United States. (1964). *Civil Rights Act of 1964.* https://www.congress.gov/bill/88th-congress/house-bill/7152

117. States, U. (1965). *Voting Rights Act of 1965.* https://www.congress.gov/bill/89th-congress/senate-bill/1564/text

118. States, U. (1986). *Immigration Reform and Control Act of 1986.* https://www.congress.gov/bill/99th-congress/senate-bill/1200

119. Security, U. S. D. of H. (2012, June 15). *Exercising Prosecutorial Discretion with Respect to Individuals Who Came to the United States as Children.* https://www.dhs.gov/xlibrary/assets/s1-exercising-prosecutorial-discretion-individuals-who-came-to-us-as-children.pdf

120. States, U. (1914). *Clayton Antitrust Act.* https://www.govinfo.gov/content/pkg/COMPS-3049/pdf/COMPS-3049.pdf

121. States, U. (1932). *Norris-LaGuardia Act.* https://www.govinfo.gov/content/pkg/COMPS-5312/pdf/COMPS-5312.pdf

122. States, U. (1935). *National Labor Relations Act*. https://www.nlrb.gov/guidance/key-reference-materials/national-labor-relations-act

123. Peterson, C. L. (2023). *Retirement Benefits for Members of Congress (No. RL30631)*. Congressional Research Service. https://crsreports.congress.gov/product/pdf/RL/RL30631

124. Intelligence, O. of the D. of N. (2024, March 11). *2024 Annual Threat Assessment of the U.S. Intelligence Community*. https://www.dni.gov/index.php/newsroom/reports-publications/reports-publications-2024/3787-2024-annual-threat-assessment-of-the-u-s-intelligence-community

125. Defense, U. S. D. of. (2024). *2024-2027 Climate Adaptation Plan*. https://www.sustainability.gov/pdfs/dod-2024-cap.pdf

126. Cho, R. (2023, October). *Why climate change is a national security risk*. https://news.climate.columbia.edu/2023/10/11/why-climate-change-is-a-national-security-risk/

127. Parsons, L., & Parsons, L. (2021, November). *How climate change will impact national security*. https://news.harvard.edu/gazette/story/2021/11/how-climate-change-will-impact-national-security/

128. Montague, P., & Woronczuk, A. (2020). *Plutocrats control the US political system, but they can still be defeated*. https://truthout.org/articles/plutocrats-control-the-us-political-system-but-they-can-still-be-defeated/

129. Lempinen, E. (2024, November). *How plutocrats, populists are driving a precarious moment in U.S. history—Berkeley News*. https://news.berkeley.edu/2020/07/10/how-plutocrats-populists-are-driving-a-precarious-moment-in-u-s-history/

130. *Would you recognize a plutocracy if you saw one?* Inequality.org. (2018, August). https://inequality.org/article/would-you-recognize-a-plutocracy-if-you-saw-one/

131. States, U. (2003). *Authorization for Use of Military Force Against Iraq Resolution of 2002*. https://www.congress.gov/107/plaws/publ243/PLAW-107publ243.pdf

132. States, U. (1948). *Foreign Assistance Act of 1948*. https://govtrackus.s3.amazonaws.com/legislink/pdf/stat/62/STATUTE-62-Pg137.pdf

133. Runde, D. F. (2024). *U.S. Foreign Assistance in the Age of Strategic Competition*. https://www.csis.org/analysis/us-foreign-assistance-age-strategic-competition

134. *USAID History | Archive—U.S. Agency for International Development*. (n.d.). https://2012-2017.usaid.gov/who-we-are/usaid-history

135. *A brief history of U.S. foreign aid.* (2023, April). https://education.cfr.org/learn/reading/brief-history-us-foreign-aid

136. Wright, M. (2025). How Much the U.S. Spent on Foreign Aid—And Where It Went. *The Wall Street Journal.* https://www.wsj.com/politics/policy/how-much-the-u-s-spent-on-foreign-aidand-where-it-went-a8c66088

137. Geiger, A. (2024). *The changing face of America's veteran population.* https://www.pewresearch.org/short-reads/2023/11/08/the-changing-face-of-americas-veteran-population/

138. Affairs, U. S. D. of V. (2024). *2024 National Veteran Suicide Prevention Annual Report* (Part 2 of 2). https://www.mentalhealth.va.gov/docs/data-sheets/2024/2024-Annual-Report-Part-2-of-2_508.pdf

139. Congress, U. S. (1944). *Servicemen's Readjustment Act of 1944.* https://www.loc.gov/law/help/statutes-at-large/78th-congress/session-2/c78s2ch268.pdf

140. Congress, U. S. (1984). *Montgomery GI Bill Active Duty* (MGIB-AD). https://www.congress.gov/bill/98th-congress/house-bill/5167

141. Congress, U. S. (2008). *Post-9/11 Veterans Educational Assistance Act of 2008.* https://www.congress.gov/bill/110th-congress/house-bill/2642

142. Huxley, A. (1932). *Brave New World.* Chatto & Windus.

143. *World Bank Open Data.* (n.d.). https://data.worldbank.org/indicator/NY.GDP.PCAP.CD?order=wbapi_data_value_2011+wbapi_data_value+wbapi_data_value-last&sort=desc

Acknowledgments

This book would not exist without the quiet encouragement and generous support of many people who, share a belief in the enduring promise of our Republic.

To David Aretha, editor, collaborator, and early believer — thank you for seeing the soul of this book from the start. Your insights, edits, and suggestions helped shape its message in ways that go far beyond grammar and structure.

To Martha Bullen, thank you for keeping the publishing process moving forward — your guidance and patience helped bring this book to life.

To Christy Day, whose creative work on the cover and interior design brought visual clarity and spirit to every page — your effort made the book not just readable, but inviting.

To Tab Scott, author, publisher, speaker, and friend — your example gave me the courage to write this. Your leadership and conviction were a spark.

To my wife, Kim, and two sons, Will and Lucas, thank you for your love, patience, and belief in me. Your support made the long hours and endless rewrites possible.

To all my friends and acquaintances — thank you for the conversations that shaped the content of this book. Every story, question, and challenge helped sharpen its voice.

And finally, to the countless citizens — past and present — whose courage and clarity built the foundation we now stand on: this book is, quite literally, for you.

About the Author

 **BILL BIVINS** is a U.S. Navy veteran, inventor, and clean energy entrepreneur with over 30 years of leadership in renewable energy, innovation, and civic systems thinking. As Founder and CEO of One World Clean Energy, Inc., he has developed technologies that eliminate landfills, reduce fossil fuel dependence, and deliver sustainable energy solutions to underserved communities.

With formal education in nuclear engineering, physics, and economics, Bill brings a rare blend of technical expertise and moral clarity to every endeavor. It was a deepening sense of political urgency, not a technical challenge, that inspired his first book.

During the 2016 election, Bill recognized patterns in American politics that echoed the warning signs of authoritarian regimes. He began rereading 1984 and Mein Kampf, and what he discovered was chilling: an unmistakable echo of authoritarian tactics playing out in real time. That realization sparked his research journey into American political history, party platforms, and systematic manipulation.

The result is *A Republic By the People*, a bold, historically grounded, and urgently relevant manifesto that challenges Americans to reclaim their republic through informed resistance and collective action.

Bill lives in Louisville, Kentucky and is a sought-after speaker on topics ranging from clean energy to civic engagement and democratic resilience. To learn more or contact Bill, visit www.linkedin.com/in/billbivins.

www.ingramcontent.com/pod-product-compliance
Lightning Source LLC
Chambersburg PA
CBHW051624120626
46551CB00014B/1931